Nicky Horne's

Viewers' Guide to American Football

ALSO PUBLISHED BY ROBSON BOOKS

and written by
Nicky Horne

The Complete American Football Book

Nicky Horne's

Viewers' Guide to
American Football

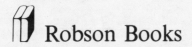 Robson Books

First published in Great Britain in 1986 by Robson Books Ltd.,
Bolsover House,   5-6 Clipstone Street,   London W1P 7EB.

British Library Cataloguing in Publication Data

Horne, Nicky
    Viewers' guide to American football.
    1. Football
    I. Title
    796.332′02′024   GV950.6

ISBN 0-86051-403-X

Made and printed in Great Britain by The Guernsey Press Co.
Ltd., Guernsey, Channel Islands.

Contents

List of Illustrations

9

Acknowledgements

My grateful thanks to all of the NFL teams who have kindly sent me their Media Guides and other useful information.

I would not have been able to compile this without the invaluable information from *The Official NFL Encyclopedia of Pro Football* and *The Official NFL Record and Fact Book 1985*.

And special thanks to Debra Shipley for all her hard work and patience in helping to turn a TV presenter into a 'writer'!

Introduction

I remember it so well. It was 5 November 1982. It was bitterly cold and I was utterly petrified. I was about to record the first-ever American Football programme for Channel Four. We were in a tiny television studio in the heart of London's Soho. Outside, the Italian restaurants and the strip bars were doing their normal business. Downstairs, in our electronic basement, you could cut the tension with a knife. It's always a nervous experience when you're in a television studio, especially in front of the camera, but when you're starting a brand-new programme and you have no idea whatsoever what the audience is going to be or how it is going to be accepted, it just increases those nerves. And boy, was I nervous!

Elaine Rose is the lady who produced the first series of American Football. She came down on to the studio floor before the cameras started rolling; she smiled, wished me good luck, checked my make-up (and believe me I need more than most) went upstairs to the control room and off we went. American Football was on the air.

All through that next week we waited with bated breath to find out if anyone had watched. And then the phone-call came from Channel Four. 1,596,000 people had watched the first transmission of American Football. The champagne corks started flying all round the Cheerleader office where the programme was produced. We were on the air and we had a hit.

But never in our wildest dreams did we imagine that four seasons on we would be picking up a regular audience of six million people and that Superbowl XX would have an audience of around twelve million. We never believed that over two hundred teams would be playing the game in this country, and that multi-national companies like Budweiser and American Express would be putting their corporate money into the development of the game in Great Britain.

11

Despite that audience of 1.5 million it was not an auspicious start. The 1982 season was reduced from a 16-game schedule to nine as a result of the 57-day players' strike. So we went on the air not with a live game but a pre-recorded game from the previous season. Still, the strike was soon over and the programme settled down to achieve a respectable and incredibly loyal audience. Our first Superbowl, Superbowl XVII, although a technical nightmare, achieved one of the highest audiences in Channel Four's brief history.

I've written this book for you if you're a regular follower of the game on Channel Four. Inside you will see each team listed with information of the team's history, the players, the coaches, how they did last year, their record against other teams in the NFL, and at the end I have included a prediction number which is my assessment of their chances of reaching the play-offs (a Richter scale of 0-10 for post-season play) — the lower the number, the less chance.

There is an end-of-season depth chart as the final item on each team. The key to it appears on page 16.

At the time of writing, the 1986 draft has not yet taken place. So therefore it has been impossible to include this year's rookies, but the book is crammed full of useful facts that you can impress your friends with. At the end we've printed the season's schedule, with space for you to write the scores as you hear them every week.

You can now consider yourself a fully qualified armchair quarterback! I hope you enjoy the season.

NICKY HORNE, MAY 1986

Structure of the National Football League

There are 28 teams in the National Football League, divided into two conferences (the American Conference and the National Conference), each with 14 teams. Both conferences are divided into three divisions: the AFC East, the AFC Central, the AFC West; the NFC East, the NFC Central, the NFC West.

AMERICAN FOOTBALL CONFERENCE	NATIONAL FOOTBALL CONFERENCE
Eastern Division	*Eastern Division*
Indianapolis Colts	Dallas Cowboys
Buffalo Bills	New York Giants
Miami Dolphins	Philadelphia Eagles
New England Patriots	St Louis Cardinals
New York Jets	Washington Redskins
Central Division	*Central Division*
Cincinnati Bengals	Chicago Bears
Cleveland Browns	Detroit Lions
Houston Oilers	Green Bay Packers
Pittsburgh Steelers	Minnesota Vikings
	Tampa Bay Buccaneers
Western Division	*Western Division*
Denver Broncos	Atlanta Falcons
Kansas City Chiefs	Los Angeles Rams
Los Angeles Raiders	New Orleans Saints
San Diego Chargers	San Francisco 49ers
Seattle Seahawks	

Each team plays 16 games during the regular season, including two games (one home, one away) against each

13

opponent within its division. The team with the best record in each division becomes division champion, and advances automatically to post-season play — the play-offs. The two teams in each conference with the next best records qualify for 'wild-card' action.

Play-off Structure

The ultimate goal for each NFL team is to win the Superbowl, and after the 16-game regular season the Division winners and the Wild Card teams compete in the play-offs in the following sequence.

The play-offs begin with the two Wild Card teams in each Conference playing each other in the first round. The winners advance to the Divisional play-offs. The winners of the Divisional play-offs advance to the Conference Championships. The winners of those two games then meet in the Superbowl.

Brief description of the Rules

Here is a real distillation of the rules of American Football. It's much more complicated than this — but read on, and you will have the basics!

Football is played by two teams. Each team has a squad of 45 players, but only 11 players from each team are allowed on the field at any one time. Each squad is subdivided into three teams: the offense, the defense and the special teams. The key on page 16 to the end-of-season depth charts at the end of each team's entry tells you more about these.

The football field is 120 yards long and 160 feet wide. At each end is the 'end zone' which is 10 yards deep — so the distance from one end zone to the other is 100 yards. The field has painted across it white lines spaced 5 yards apart.

Football, like rugby, is a territorial game — the object being to advance into your opponents' territory, eventually getting into the end zone for a 'touchdown', which is worth six points. Another point can be added after a touchdown if the ball is then kicked from the two-yard line through the goal posts. This is called a P.A.T. ('point after touchdown'). Other ways of gaining points are through the 'field goal' by kicking the ball between an opponent's goal posts, and worth three points, and through the 'safety', which gives two points to the defensive team when an offensive team player downs the ball behind his own goal line.

To advance up the field the team with the ball ('the offense') use the 'down system', which works like this: the offense is given four attempts to move the ball at least 10 yards. If they succeed in moving it 10 yards or more, then they get another four goes, and so on. If, for instance, on their first attempt they achieve only four yards, so that they have six yards still to make from their initial target of 10, they then have their second attempt (that's called 'second and six'). If on their second and third attempts they still do not make the necessary six yards, then on their fourth and final attempt (unless they're within field goal range) they will 'punt' the ball to the opposition. That means they will kick it as far into opposition territory as possible, thus making their opponents regain possession deep in their own half of the field.

SCORING:

Field goal	3 points
Touchdown	6 points
P.A.T.	1 point
Safety	2 points

Key to end-of-season depth charts

OFFENSE

WR	—	wide receiver
T	—	tackle
OLT	—	offensive left tackle
G	—	guard
OLG	—	offensive left guard
C	—	center
ORG	—	offensive right guard
ORT	—	offensive right tackle
TE	—	tight end
QB	—	quarterback
H-B	—	halfback
RB	—	running back

SPECIAL TEAMS

P	—	punter
K	—	kicker
H	—	holder
PR	—	punt returner
KR	—	kick returner
LSN	—	long snapper
LSN(P)	—	punting center
LSN(F)	—	field goal center

DEFENSE

DE	—	defensive end
DLE	—	defensive left end
DT	—	defensive tackle
DLT	—	defensive left tackle
NT	—	nose tackle
MG	—	middle guard
DRT	—	defensive right tackle
DRE	—	defensive right end
LB	—	linebacker
LOLB	—	left outside linebacker
LLB	—	left linebacker
LILB	—	left inside linebacker
MLB	—	middle linebacker
RILB	—	right inside linebacker
RLB	—	right linebacker
ROLB	—	right outside linebacker
CB	—	cornerback
LCB	—	left cornerback
RCB	—	right cornerback
S	—	safety
SS	—	strong safety
LS	—	left safety
FS	—	free safety
RS	—	right safety

16

American Football Conference

Buffalo Bills

AMERICAN FOOTBALL CONFERENCE — EASTERN DIVISION

Address:	One Bills Drive, Orchard Park, New York 14127
Telephone:	(716) 648-1800
Colours:	Royal blue, scarlet red, and white
Stadium:	Rich Stadium, One Bills Drive, Orchard Park, New York 14127
Capacity:	80,290
Playing surface:	AstroTurf

History

The original Buffalo Bill was William Cody, the archetypal American showman who claimed to have killed 4,280 buffalo to feed the builders of the Kansas Pacific Railroad. The team who took his name have yet to emulate his prowess or his showmanship, seeing play-off action only eight times since 1963, and not once representing the AFC in the Superbowl.

The Bills, however, did for a time have an athlete of outstanding ability who put Buffalo on the football map and who drew the crowds in the thousands to their home games, and in their millions to their TV sets. His name was O.J. Simpson. 'The Juice' was until 1977 *the* Buffalo Bill.

In 1969 Simpson was selected by Buffalo as their first choice in the draft. Fresh from winning the Heisman Trophy for Excellence in College Football, Simpson made sure his agent negotiated hard, and a month after training camp opened O.J. signed a long-term deal with the Bills. It was not immediately

19

apparent that the Bills had got such a great deal as Simpson was disappointing in his first two seasons — but in 1972 he had his first 1,000-yard season and was named the AFC's Player of the Year.

On 29 October 1973 at New York's Shea Stadium in a dramatic final game of the season Simpson ran for 200 yards and in finishing the season with 2,003 yards he rushed into the record books by breaking Jim Brown's 10-year-old rushing record. In 1974 the Bills finished the season 9-5 and advanced to the AFC divisional play-off where they were walloped by the Pittsburgh Steelers 32-14.

1976 was an awful year, and even with a change of coaches halfway through the season, the Bills finished with a miserable two wins and 12 losses. 1977 wasn't much better. Their record then was three wins, 11 losses, including three shut-outs to the Miami Dolphins, the Atlanta Falcons and the Washington Redskins. It was in 1980 that the Bills started winning again. Their record of 11 and five made them AFC Eastern Division Champions, but in the Divisional play-offs they lost to the San Diego Chargers 20-14. Chuck Knox had been their coach since 1978 and 1981 was his best year. In the Wild Card game on 27 December 1981 the Bills beat the New York Jets narrowly 31-27, but in the Divisional play-off game they lost to the Cincinnati Bengals 21-28. Knox had one more year. In the strike-shortened season of 1982 they won four and lost five, and lost Chuck Knox. Coach Kay Stephenson replaced Knox and managed an eight and eight record in 1983, but 1984 was a disaster. They lost 14 and could win only two. There was scant satisfaction that one of those wins was over the Dallas Cowboys on 18 November, the other against Indianapolis Colts on 2 December.

Last season

Up in the frozen north, the Bills are still waiting for a thaw in their fortunes. Last year's 2-14 campaign, during which time coach Kay Stephenson was asked to leave, was just about rock bottom, as those two wins came over Houston and Indianapolis.

At quarterback the Vince Ferragamo experiment was a flop,

Buffalo Bills vs NFL

	Won	Lost	Tied
Atlanta	2	2	0
Chicago	1	2	0
Cincinnati	5	8	0
Cleveland	2	5	0
Dallas	1	3	0
Denver	13	9	1
Detroit	1	1	1
Green Bay	2	1	0
Houston	9	17	0
Indianapolis	15	15	1
Kansas City	14	11	1
Los Angeles Raiders	11	12	0
Los Angeles Rams	1	3	0
Miami	7	32	1
Minnesota	1	4	0
New England	23	28	1
New Orleans	2	1	0
New York Giants	1	2	0
New York Jets	26	25	0
Philadelphia	1	3	0
Pittsburgh	3	6	0
San Diego	91	17	2
San Francisco	2	1	0
St Louis	1	3	0
Seattle	0	2	0
Tampa Bay	1	2	0
Washington	2	2	0

so new boy Bruce Mathison had a chance to strut his stuff, and he certainly learnt how to scramble quickly! Greg Bell once again carried the offense as Buffalo struggled with both the run and the pass.

End-of-season depth chart

OFFENSE

WR	—	80 Jerry Butler, 82 Eric Richardson, 86 Jimmy Teal
OLT	—	72 Ken Jones, 63 Justin Cross
OLG	—	51 Jim Ritcher, 62 Mark Traynowicz
C	—	53 Will Grant, 65 Tim Vogler, 62 Mark Traynowicz
ORG	—	65 Tim Vogler, 69 Greg Christy
ORT	—	70 Joe Devlin, 63 Justin Cross
TE	—	87 Eason Ramson, 88 Pete Metzelaars
WR	—	83 Andre Reed, 85 Chris Burkett
QB	—	7 Bruce Mathison, 14 Frank Reich
RB	—	28 Greg Bell, 20 Joe Cribbs
RB	—	34 Booker Moore, 45 Anthony Steels

DEFENSE

DLE	—	77 Ben Williams, 95 Sean McNanie, 79 Dean Prater
NT	—	76 Fred Smerlas, 74 Don Smith
DRE	—	78 Bruce Smith, 74 Don Smith
LOLB	—	52 Guy Frazier, 56 Darryl Talley
LILB	—	54 Eugene Marve, 90 Steve Maidlow
RILB	—	55 Jim Haslett, 50 Eric Wilson
ROLB	—	57 Lucius Sanford, 58 Anthony Dickerson
LCB	—	29 Derrick Burroughs, 48 Lawrence Johnson, 25 Rod Hill
RCB	—	26 Charles Romes, 36 Rodney Bellinger
SS	—	22 Steve Freeman, 21 Donald Wilson
FS	—	21 Donald Wilson, 23 Jim Perryman

SPECIAL TEAMS

P	—	4 John Kidd
K	—	11 Scott Norwood
H	—	4 John Kidd
PR	—	25 Rod Hill, 45 Anthony Steels, 21 Donald Wilson
KR	—	21 Donald Wilson, 45 Anthony Steels, 82 Eric Richardson
LSN	—	50 Eric Wilson, 63 Justin Cross, 53 Will Grant

ALSO WITH THE BUFFALO BILLS
Chris Babyar (G), 43 Martin Bayless (S),
81 Mitchell Brookins (WR), 59 Stan David (LB),
99 Hal Garner (LB), Mike Hamby (NT), Bo Harris (LB),
71 Dale Hellestrae (T), 30 Anthony Hutchison (RB), Ron Pitts
(CB), 40 Robb Riddick (RB), James Seawright (LB)

It was the same story on defense as well. First round picked Bruce Smith added little to a lacklustre outfit, although the secondary played with pride forcing most opponents to opt for a running game.

Prediction

New coach Hank Bullough knows that the road back from consecutive 2-14 seasons is steep and treacherous. In the 'giveaway-takeaway' department which Bullough reckons is one of the most important barometers, the Bills ranked 28th in the League with a –17. In other words, Buffalo gave the ball to their opponents 17 more times than they took it away. Buffalo were also called for 132 infractions, more than any other team in the League. Bullough has his work cut out: they will be very lucky not to have a losing season again.

Play-off prediction

0

Cincinnati Bengals

AMERICAN FOOTBALL CONFERENCE — CENTRAL DIVISION

Address:	200 River Front Stadium, Cincinnati, Ohio 45202
Telephone:	(513) 621-3550
Colours:	Black, orange and white
Stadium:	River Front Stadium, Cincinnati, Ohio 45202
Capacity:	59,754
Playing surface:	AstroTurf

History

There was a team called the Bengals back in 1937 in the old AFL but it was not until 27 October 1967 that the Bengals were officially named as an expansion team in the AFL, and on 15 September 1968, in their first home game, they had an auspicious start by defeating Denver 24-10. In the 1970 season Cincinnati slaughtered Boston 45-7 and won the Central Division Championship of the American Football Conference. It was in front of the largest sports crowd in Cincinnati history, over 60,000.

It was in 1981 that the Bengals adopted the now familiar uniform of tiger-strip helmets, playing shirts and pants, and it did them the power of good. They had their best-ever season, 12 wins, four losses. On 3 January 1982 they beat Buffalo 28-21 and a week later they won their first ever AFC Championship, beating San Diego 27-7. Their quarterback Ken Anderson led

25

them to victory in spite of the appalling weather conditions; with the wind chill factor it was an unbelievable –59° at River Front Stadium that day.

On 24 January 1982 they met the 49ers in Superbowl XV and at half time were 20-0 down, but despite a thrilling second half the Bengals lost 26-21.

On 26 December 1982 the Bengals clinched a play-off berth by beating Seattle 24-10, but went down to the New York Jets 44-17 in the first round of the play-offs.

The 1984 season didn't start well for the Bengals, 0 and 5, but under coach Sam Wyche they finished with a relatively respectable record of 8 and 8.

The Bengals' mascot is an Indian white tiger called Benzoo and he appears at each home game. Funny thing, they don't take him on the road!

Last season

The enigmatic Bengals once again astounded NFL watchers. The same team that could rack up 50 points with ease against Dallas would also allow Houston's impotent offense to score 44. At least Boomer Esiason's number 7 confirmed his arrival as starting quarterback ahead of old-stager Ken Anderson. Last season Esiason was number 9 in the top 10 of quarterbacks with 27 touchdowns. This 25-year-old left-hander is a smart and competent quarterback who doesn't mind running. By the way, if you wondered how he got his nickname of Boomer, it's derived from two sources. Apparently when he was still in his mother's womb he kicked a great deal and, since a kicker at his father's school had been known as 'Boomer', his parents called him Boomer! And it stuck, poor chap. Last season the free-spirited Esiason spent much of his time throwing to Cris Collingsworth, Rookie of the Year (offense), Eddie Brown and the surprisingly effective T.E. Rodney Holman, and when it wasn't in the air the ball would be in the safe hands of running backs James Brooks and Larry Kinnebrew.

But while the offense was well balanced, the defense was unstable, especially against the well-thrown pass, and coach Sam Wyche's team never conceded fewer than ten points.

26

Cincinnati Bengals vs NFL

	Won	Lost	Tied
Atlanta	4	1	0
Buffalo	8	5	0
Chicago	2	0	0
Cleveland	16	15	0
Dallas	1	2	0
Denver	6	8	0
Detroit	1	2	0
Green Bay	3	2	0
Houston	20	13	1
Indianapolis	4	5	0
Kansas City	7	8	0
Los Angeles Raiders	4	12	0
Los Angeles Rams	3	2	0
Miami	3	7	0
Minnesota	2	2	0
New England	3	6	0
New Orleans	3	2	0
New York Giants	3	0	0
New York Jets	3	7	0
Philadelphia	4	0	0
Pittsburgh	14	17	0
San Diego	7	10	0
San Francisco	1	4	0
St Louis	2	1	0
Seattle	3	2	0
Tampa Bay	2	1	0
Washington	1	3	0

Prediction

At the end of last season Cincinnati finished with a record of 7 and 9, second in the AFC Central to Cleveland. I would expect

End-of-season depth chart

OFFENSE

WR	—	80 Cris Collinsworth, 88 Mike Martin
OLT	—	78 Anthony Munoz, 75 Bruce Reimers
OLG	—	74 Brian Blados, 64 Bruce Kozerski
C	—	52 Dave Rimington, 64 Bruce Kozerski
ORG	—	65 Max Montoya, 64 Bruce Kozerski
ORT	—	77 Mike Wilson, 63 Joe Walter
TE	—	82 Rodney Holman, 83 M.L. Harris
WR	—	81 Eddie Brown, 86 Steve Kreider, 87 Pat Mcinally
QB	—	7 Boomer Esiason, 15 Turk Schonert, 14 Ken Anderson
RB	—	21 James Brooks, 36 Stanford Jennings
RB	—	28 Larry Kinnebrew, 40 Charles Alexander, 30 Bill Johnson

DEFENSE

DLE	—	73 Eddie Edwards, 76 Glen Collins
NT	—	69 Tim Krumrie, 61 Jerry Boyarsky
DRE	—	79 Ross Browner, 76 Glen Collins
LOLB	—	59 Jeff Schuh, 53 Leo Barker
LILB	—	56 Ron Simpkins, 91 Carl Zander
RILB	—	50 Glenn Cameron, 91 Carl Zander, Tom Dinkel
ROLB	—	57 Reggie Williams, 90 Emanuel King
LCB	—	34 Louis Breeden, 25 John Simmons
RCB	—	20 Ray Horton, 35 Jimmy Turner, Sam Washington
SS	—	26 Bobby Kemp, 22 James Griffin
FS	—	22 James Griffin, 37 Robert Jackson

SPECIAL TEAMS

P	—	87 Pat Mcinally
K	—	3 Jim Breech
H	—	86 Steve Kreider
PR	—	88 Mike Martin, 25 John Simmons
KR	—	88 Mike Martin, 36 Stanford Jennings
LSN	—	64 Bruce Kozerski, 52 Dave Rimington

ALSO WITH THE CINCINNATI BENGALS
89 Don Kern (TE)

them to do better this year as Esiason gains more confidence, and if Wyche can shore up the defense they could top the AFC Central this time around.

Play-off prediction

6

Cleveland Browns

AMERICAN FOOTBALL CONFERENCE — CENTRAL DIVISION

Address:	Tower B, Cleveland Stadium, Cleveland, Ohio 44114
Telephone:	(216) 696-5555
Colours:	Seal brown, orange and white
Stadium:	Cleveland Stadium, West 3rd Street, Cleveland, Ohio 44114
Capacity:	80,093
Playing surface:	Grass

History

Arthur McBride was a man who in 1946 was doing very nicely, thank you. He owned a couple of cab companies, a printing company, a radio station, a race wire service, and had acres of real estate. But McBride was not content, he now wanted a football team — he also needed a name for his new acquisition. McBride offered a $1,000 War Bond to the fan who came up with the best name. One of the 36 entrants — a naval man, John Harnett — thought of the name 'The Panthers'. But in the 1920s there had been an NFL team in Cleveland called the Panthers who had been a miserable failure, and the name was rejected. But a large majority of the remaining 35 fans had suggested the name 'Browns', in recognition of the newly-appointed coach, Paul Brown. With characteristic modesty Brown turned down the idea initially: 'You can't name a team after their coach.' But after some fierce arm-twisting Paul Brown was persuaded, and thus became the only man in professional football to have a team named after him. Brown personally selected the team colours, and in their first season they beat the Miami Seahawks 44-0 at Cleveland Stadium and then won seven in a row before losing to the San Francisco 49ers.

In 1951-53 the Browns won three consecutive Eastern Division titles, but lost each time in the title match. In 1953 McBride sold the club for $600,000, the highest price ever paid for a pro football franchise. So important to the new owners was coach Paul Brown that they took out a massive insurance policy on his life, as they regarded him as the team's biggest asset.

In 1957, Brown wanted to draft a quarterback, but for that they had to wait until the second round. In the first round they got a man who was to become a legend in the NFL, Jim Brown. Four games into the season Brown ran 237 yards for a new NFL record, and although the Browns won the Eastern Division title they were defeated by the Lions in the championship game. But Jim Brown, already showing his greatness, was named Rookie of the Year.

In 1964 the Browns won a divisional title from the Giants, and won the NFL Championship with a 27-0 win over the Colts. In 1970 the Browns became members of the AFC Central and ended up in second place, and the following year they won the AFC Central. In 1972 they saw the playoffs again, but lost to Miami who went on to become champions. In 1980 the Browns again won the AFC Central but lost to Oakland in the playoffs.

Last season

You have to admire what coach Marty Schottenheimer has achieved in less than two seasons. Before a hostile Miami crowd, they raced to a 21-3 lead in a play-off game against the Dolphins before running out of steam.

That match saw the power of the Browns' running game, which combines Earnest Byner and Kevin Mack (Both 1,000 yard men last year), with the explosive speed of Curtis Dickey. Add to this the promise of rookie QB Bernie Kosar, and you can see why NFL observers started looking closely at Cleveland last year.

32

Cleveland Browns vs NFL

	Won	Lost	Tied
Atlanta	6	1	0
Buffalo	5	2	0
Chicago	6	2	0
Cincinnati	15	16	0
Dallas	15	9	0
Denver	3	8	0
Detroit	3	12	0
Green Bay	5	7	0
Houston	20	11	0
Indianapolis	10	5	0
Kansas City	4	5	1
Los Angeles Raiders	1	9	0
Los Angeles Rams	8	7	0
Miami	3	3	0
Minnesota	1	7	0
New England	6	2	0
New Orleans	8	1	0
New York Giants	26	16	2
New York Jets	7	3	0
Philadelphia	29	11	1
Pittsburgh	41	31	0
San Diego	4	5	1
San Francisco	8	4	0
St Louis	30	10	3
Seattle	2	7	0
Tampa Bay	3	0	0
Washington	31	8	1

True, they only finished 8-8 on the regular season, but with the introduction of a couple of quick receivers, they'd be a match for anyone. Watch them lay a claim to a Superbowl spot in 1986.

End-of-season depth chart

OFFENSE

WR	— 85 Clarence Weathers, 83 Fred Banks, 84 Glen Young
OLT	— 74 Paul Farren, 77 Rickey Bolden, 75 Bill Contz
OLG	— 62 George Lilja, 68 Robert Jackson
C	— 61 Mike Baab, 62 George Lilja
ORG	— 69 Dan Fike, 77 Rickey Bolden, 68 Robert Jackson
ORT	— 63 Cody Risien, 77 Rickey Bolden, 75 Bill Contz
TE	— 82 Ozzie Newsome, 81 Harry Holt, 87 Travis Tucker
WR	— 86 Brian Brennan, 88 Reggie Langhorne
QB	— 19 Bernie Kosar, 18 Gary Danielson, 16 Paul McDonald
RB	— 44 Earnest Byner, 30 Boyce Green, 28 Herman Fontenot
RB	— 34 Kevin Mack, 38 Johnny Davis, 33 Curtis Dickey

DEFENSE

DLE	— 96 Reggie Camp, 72 Dave Puzzuoli
NT	— 79 Bob Golic, 72 Dave Puzzuoli
DRE	— 78 Carl Hairston, 91 Sam Clancy, 99 Keith Baldwin
LOLB	— 56 Chip Banks, 55 Curtis Weathers
LILB	— 51 Eddie Johnson, 58 Scott Nicolas
RILB	— 50 Tom Cousineau, 58 Scott Nicolas
ROLB	— 57 Clay Matthews, 55 Curtis Weathers
LCB	— 31 Frank Minnifield, 47 Larry Braziel
RCB	— 29 Hanford Dixon, 47 Larry Braziel
SS	— 27 Al Gross, 37 Chris Rockins
FS	— 20 Don Rogers, 22 Felix Wright

SPECIAL TEAMS

P	— 7 Jeff Gossett, 9 Matt Bahr
K	— 9 Matt Bahr
H	— 16 Paul McDonald, 7 Jeff Gossett, 18 Gary Danielson
PR	— 86 Brian Brennan, 85 Clarence Weathers
KR	— 84 Glen Young, 28 Herman Fontenot, 85 Clarence Weathers
LSN	— 58 Scott Nicolas, 74 Paul Farren, 62 George Lilja

ALSO WITH THE CLEVELAND BROWNS
80 Willis Adams (WR-TE), 26 Greg Allen (RB), Terry Brooks (T),
49 Clinton Burrell (S), 39 Eddie Colson (RB), Troy Hill (DB),
97 David Morrill (DE), Stan Shakespeare (WR),
Brian Vogt (DE), 70 Larry Williams (G)

Prediction

'We have one goal in 1986, and that is to win the Superbowl. Anything else will not be satisfying. We don't have intermediate goals. Making the play-offs or winning a certain number of games becomes unimportant if the last game you play in the season is a loss. We did, however, make improvements last year and it was an education for me. With the tough play-off loss to the Dolphins, as well as some of the other close games we dropped, I sense a resolve among our players. We all have a better understanding of the small margins that exist between winning and losing in the NFL. We are committed to win this year and we have the energy to make it happen.' So said Marti Schottenheimer earlier this year. If he can instil that attitude into his team this coming season the Browns should see play-off action.

Play-off prediction

6

Denver Broncos

AMERICAN FOOTBALL CONFERENCE — WESTERN DIVISION

Address:	5700 Logan Street, Denver, Colorado 80216
Telephone:	(303) 296-1982
Colours:	Orange, blue and white
Stadium:	Mile High Stadium, 1900 West Eliot, Denver, Colorado 80204
Capacity:	75,100
Playing surface:	Grass

History

The Broncos were born on 14 August 1959 as Charter members of the American Football League. They were put into the AFC's Western Division along with the Oakland Raiders, the Los Angeles Chargers and the Dallas Texans. On 9 September 1960 they defeated the Patriots 13-10 in the first AFL game in history — a crowd of 21,000 saw them do it.

In 1962 the team's vertically-striped socks, which were hated by fans and players alike, were ceremoniously burned at a specially-convened public gathering! It must have been lucky — in their first regular season game, minus those socks, they beat San Diego for the first time: 30-21.

The year 1965 was a bad one for the Broncos. The crowds started to fall away and the owners, convinced that the Broncos had no future, decided to sell. The Cox Broadcasting Company made a $4-million offer and announced it would move the franchise to Atlanta. This threat that the Broncos would leave town did wonderful things to their attendance and ticket sales miraculously boomed.

On 4 December 1977 the Broncos beat Houston 24-14 to clinch a play-off spot — the first in the club's history, and later in the day when the Raiders were beaten by the Rams they became AFC Western Division Champions.

On 24 December 1977, in front of 75,000 people, the largest crowd ever to watch a sporting event in the state of Colorado, the Broncos defeated the Pittsburgh Steelers in the first round of the play-offs, 34-21. Despite defeating the Raiders in the AFC Championship game, the Broncos lost to the Cowboys 27-10 at the Louisiana Superdome in Superbowl XII. The Broncos didn't go home empty-handed. On that day each member of the losing team collected $9,000 — it was double that for each of the victorious Cowboys.

In 1979 Denver saw post-season action again but on 23 December they lost in a Wild Card play-off game at Houston 13-7.

On 2 May 1983, in the biggest trade in franchise history, Denver signed young quarterback John Elway — $6 million was his fee for a five-year contract. Elway's debut in the NFL was not what you would expect from the 'six-million-dollar man' but after a slow and insecure start, on 11 December he threw three fourth-quarter touchdown passes to reverse a 19-0 deficit and led the Broncos to a 21-19 play-off spot by beating Baltimore. However, in the Broncos' fourth appearance in play-off competition they lost the Wild Cat game at Seattle 31-7.

On 18 November 1984, the Broncos beat Minnesota 42-21 with John Elway throwing five touchdown passes in that game. They won the AFC West and got their revenge over Seattle 31-14, but fell in the Divisional play-off game to the Steelers 24-17.

Last season

Step forward the unluckiest team in the NFL! Denver finished with a record of 11-5, but would have been even better had they not lost twice in overtime to the Raiders, and they failed to go to the play-offs.

On a brighter note, quarterback John Elway put his troubles

Denver Broncos vs NFL

	Won	Lost	Tied
Atlanta	3	3	0
Buffalo	9	13	1
Chicago	3	4	0
Cincinnati	8	6	0
Cleveland	8	3	0
Dallas	1	3	0
Detroit	3	2	0
Green Bay	3	1	0
Houston	10	18	1
Indianapolis	6	1	0
Kansas City	18	33	0
Los Angeles Raiders	13	36	2
Los Angeles Rams	2	3	0
Miami	2	5	1
Minnesota	2	2	0
New England	11	12	0
New Orleans	4	0	0
New York Giants	2	1	0
New York Jets	10	10	1
Philadelphia	1	3	0
Pittsburgh	7	5	1
San Diego	24	27	1
San Francisco	3	2	0
St Louis	1	0	1
Seattle	11	7	0
Tampa Bay	2	0	0
Washington	1	2	0

behind him and showed his fellow players, the media and the fans that he's a better than average performer. He is surrounded by players who are competent, although not really capable of doing something spectacular.

End-of-season depth chart

OFFENSE

WR	— 82 Vance Johnson, 84 Clint Sampson
OLT	— 70 Dave Studdard, 63 Mark Cooper, 67 Dean Miraldi
OLG	— 54 Keith Bishop, 74 Winford Hood, 67 Dean Miraldi, 63 Mark Cooper
C	— 64 Billy Bryan, 54 Keith Bishop
ORG	— 60 Paul Howard, 74 Winford Hood, 67 Dean Miraldi
ORT	— 76 Ken Lanier, 63 Mark Cooper
TE	— 88 Clarence Kay, 85 Mike Barber
WR	— 81 Steve Watson, 86 Butch Johnson
QB	— 7 John Elway, 8 Gary Kubiak
RB	— 23 Sammy Winder, 47 Gerald Willhite, 34 Nathan Poole, 30 Steve Sewell
HB	— 87 James Wright, 85 Mike Barber

DEFENSE

DLE	— 79 Barney Chavous, 61 Andre Townsend, 77 Karl Mecklenburg
NT	— 68 Rubin Carter, 71 Greg Kragen
DRE	— 75 Rulon Jones, 73 Simon Fletcher
LOLB	— 50 Jim Ryan, 77 Karl Mecklenburg, 59 Darren Comeaux
LILB	— 77 Karl Mecklenburg, 55 Rick Dennison, 98 Ricky Hunley
RILB	— 58 Steve Busick, 77 Karl Mecklenburg
ROLB	— 57 Tom Jackson, 52 Ken Woodard
LCB	— 20 Louis Wright, 45 Steve Wilson, 25 Daniel Hunter
RCB	— 31 Mike Harden, 45 Steve Wilson, 25 Daniel Hunter
SS	— 49 Dennis Smith, 48 Randy Robbins
FS	— 43 Steve Foley, 22 Tony Lilly

SPECIAL TEAMS

P	— 1 Chris Norman
K	— 3 Rich Karlis
H	— 8 Gary Kubiak
PR	— 47 Gerald Willhite, 82 Vance Johnson
KR	— 82 Vance Johnson, 25 Daniel Hunter
LSN	— 54 Keith Bishop, 64 Billy Bryan

ALSO WITH THE DENVER BRONCOS
62 Mike Freeman (G), 72 Marsharne Graves (T), Al Hill (WR),
51 Billy Hinson (G), 33 Gene Lang (RB), 21 Eric Riley (CB),
83 John Sawyer (TE), 56 Aaron Smith (LB), Larry Willis (WR)

On defense, linebacker-cum-nose tackle Karl Mecklenburg was given a roving brief by coach Dan Reeves, and revelled in his new role. Many were the times he would appear out of nowhere to frustrate a play. Kicker Rich Carless gave Bronco fans collective heart failure with his habit of scraping the post with his kicks, and he'll be asked to improve his accuracy. Denver do not have many talented individuals (Elway excepted) yet few teams possess such strength in depth. They'll be back!

Prediction

I have a sneaking feeling that the fans at Mile High Stadium will at last have their loyalty rewarded this coming season. If Elway stays healthy then Denver, who are always capable of big plays, should see some post-season action.

Play-off prediction

7

Houston Oilers

AMERICAN FOOTBALL CONFERENCE — CENTRAL DIVISION

Address:	Box 1516, Houston, Texas 77001
Telephone:	(713) 797-9111
Colours:	Columbia blue, scarlet and white
Stadium:	Astrodome, Loop 610, Kirby and Fannin Streets, Houston, Texas 77054
Capacity:	50,496
Playing surface:	AstroTurf

History

Houston oilman (surprise, surprise!), K.S. Bud Adams announced Houston's entry into the American Football League on 3 August 1959. And on 31 October 1959 'for sentimental and social reasons' Adams named the team the Oilers. The Oilers' first head coach was Lou Rymkus, and on 20 February 1960 the Oilers lured away from the Chicago Bears the great veteran quarterback George Blander. It was a good first season in 1960, the Oilers were 10-4, scored 379 points, and by beating Buffalo 31-23 they secured the AFL's Eastern Division title. The Oilers won the first AFL Championship, beating the Los Angeles Chargers, and Blander showed his brilliance, completing 16 of 32 passes for 301 yards and three touchdowns. The players' wages that day: $1,016.32 cents!

In 1961, the Oilers gained 10 successive victories and became the first team to score more than 500 points in a season, and they again won the AFL title, beating the San Diego Chargers 10-3. Going from strength to strength, in 1962 they won their third Eastern Division title, but in the AFL title game in an historic *six* quarter, double overtime, game, they lost 20-17 to the Dallas Texans.

Ten years later things were *very* different. On 1 October 1972 the Oilers surprised themselves, and the whole country, by defeating the great Joe Namath and the New York Jets 26-20 — the surprise was it was their *only* victory of the 1972 season! And in 1974 the Oilers announced a record loss of $459,281.

In 1975, with Bun Phillips as head coach, the Oilers had their best season with a 10-4 record. In their campaign of 1978, it looked as if the Oilers would go all the way. On 24 December in the AFC Wild Card game, Houston stunned Miami with a 17-9 win and advanced to the AFC Divisional play-offs. They travelled to Schaefer Stadium, Foxborough — the home of the Patriots — and soundly walloped them 31-14. They were one game away from representing the AFC in Superbowl XIII, but in the AFC Championship game at Three Rivers Stadium, on 7 January 1979, they lost 34-5 to the eventual Superbowl champions the Pittsburgh Steelers. It was the same story the following season. They beat Denver and San Diego in the Wild Card and Divisional play-off games respectively, but fell once again to Pittsburgh in the AFC Championship game, going down 27-13.

Their record since then makes sorry reading. In the strike-shortened 1982 season they could only manage one win, and in 1983, after six games, coach Ed Biles was replaced by Chuck Studley but they still lost 14 and won only two. They had a new coach, Hugh Campbell, for the 1984 season, but they could only muster a 3-13 record.

Last season

When the Oilers went to Miami and won the season opener, and followed that up with a desperately close loss to Washington, we all sat up and took note. Did Houston really mean business this time?

Sadly for long-suffering Oiler fans, the answer was again an emphatic no. The campaign, which began with high hopes,

44

Houston Oilers vs NFL

	Won	Lost	Tied
Atlanta	1	4	0
Buffalo	17	9	0
Chicago	2	1	0
Cincinnati	13	20	1
Cleveland	11	20	0
Dallas	1	4	0
Denver	18	10	1
Detroit	2	1	0
Green Bay	2	2	0
Indianapolis	3	5	0
Kansas City	12	20	0
Los Angeles Raiders	10	21	0
Los Angeles Rams	1	3	0
Miami	10	9	0
Minnesota	1	2	0
New England	13	14	1
New Orleans	2	2	1
New York Giants	0	3	0
New York Jets	15	10	1
Philadelphia	0	3	0
Pittsburgh	9	24	0
San Diego	12	16	1
San Francisco	2	3	0
St Louis	1	3	0
Seattle	3	2	0
Tampa Bay	2	1	0
Washington	2	2	0

ended 5-11 and earned the dismissal of coach Hugh Campbell.
Quarterback Warren Moon was clearly still learning the ways of
the NFL, and it was pretty obvious that the rest of the offense
were still learning about each other, though Drew Hill and

45

End-of-season depth chart

OFFENSE

WR — 83 Tim Smith, 82 Willie Drewrey
OLT — 73 Harvey Salem, 76 Eric Moran
OLG — 63 Mike Munchak, 66 Pat Howell, 58 Mike Kelley
C — 55 Jim Romano, 58 Mike Kelley
ORG — 62 John Schuhmacher, 70 Dean Steinkuhler, 58 Mike Kelley
ORT — 74 Bruce Matthews, 76 Eric Moran
TE — 87 Jamie Williams, 88 Chris Dressel, 89 Mike McCloskey
WR — 85 Drew Hill, 84 Herkie Walls
QB — 1 Warren Moon, 10 Oliver Luck
RB — 33 Mike Rozier, 32 Stan Edwards
RB — 40 Butch Woolfolk, 30 Larry Moriarty

DEFENSE

DLE — 79 Ray Childress, 71 Richard Byrd, 99 Doug Smith
MG — 67 Mike Stensrud, 99 Doug Smith, 72 Brian Sochia
DRE — 75 Jesse Baker, 71 Richard Byrd, 99 Doug Smith
LOLB — 93 Robert Lyles, 92 Tom Briehl
LILB — 53 Avon Riley, 59 John Grimsley
RILB — 56 Robert Abraham, 59 John Grimsley
ROLB — 94 Frank Bush, 92 Tom Briehl
LCB — 24 Steve Brown, 23 Richard Johnson, 26 Audrey McMillian
RCB — 29 Patrick Allen, 23 Richard Johnson,
26 Audrey McMillian
SS — 25 Keith Bostic, 31 Jeff Donaldson
FS — 21 Bo Eason, 37 Rod Kush, 28 Allen Lyday

SPECIAL TEAMS

P — 11 Lee Johnson, 83 Tim Smith
K — 7 Tony Zendejas, 11 Lee Johnson
H — 11 Lee Johnson, 83 Tim Smith
PR — 82 Willie Drewrey, 84 Herkie Walls
KR — 82 Willie Drewrey, 84 Herkie Walls
LSN — 74 Bruce Matthews, 55 Jim Romano

ALSO WITH THE HOUSTON OILERS
86 Mike Akiu (WR), 42 Dwayne Crutchfield (RB),
68 Mike Golic (DE), Frank Hare (MG), 97 Mike Johnson (DE),
91 Johnny Meads (LB), 80 Steve Tasker (WR/KR)

Butch Woolfolk inspired some hope; the defense, however, inspired quite the opposite. They played like a team of strangers for most of the season, and it became increasingly clear as the season progressed that the Oilers are still a team in transition.

Prediction

Not this year... not even next...

Play-off prediction

0

Indianapolis Colts

AMERICAN FOOTBALL CONFERENCE — EASTERN DIVISION

Address: PO Box 5400, Indianapolis, Indiana 46254

Telephone: (317) 252-2658

Colours: Royal blue, white, and silver

Stadium: Hoosier Dome, 100 South Capitol Avenue, Indianapolis, Indiana 46225

Capacity: 60,127

Playing surface: AstroTurf

History

On 27 March 1984 they were the Baltimore Colts. On 28 March 1984 they packed their bags, moved out of town and became the Indianapolis Colts. Baltimore, a town rock singer Nils Lofgren hated so much he wrote a song vowing he would never go back, had lost its football team overnight. While Baltimore sulked, Indianapolis went wild and there were 143,000 season ticket requests within fourteen days.

Back to the beginning, though. On 28 December 1946 the then-bankrupt Miami Seahawks franchise of the All American Football Conference moved to Baltimore. As a result of a contest in Baltimore, the team was renamed the Colts. The All American Football Conference and the National Football League merged in 1950, and the Colts duly became members of the NFL. But after two dismal years winning only two games, the franchise was dissolved. There then followed two seasons

49

without football for the luckless Baltimore fans. Two years without football did wonderful things to concentrate the mind and after a challenge by the Commissioner of the NFL, who said he would allow a franchise in Baltimore if 15,000 season tickets could be sold in six weeks, the fans responded by buying all 15,000 in four weeks and three days.

Before their first NFL season the Colts did a deal with the Cleveland Browns, involving no fewer than 15 players — *they* helped the Colts start the 1953 season with a surprising 13-9 win over the Chicago Bears. (Playing defense in that game was a young man called Don Shula.)

On 30 November 1958 the Colts got their first Western Division title, beating San Francisco 35-27. Four weeks later the Colts won their first World Championship, beating the Giants 23-17. In 1959 they clinched their second Western Division title and won the World title against the Giants 31-16.

In 1963 genius arrived in Baltimore as Don Shula became the Colts' head coach. Working with the legendary Johnny Unitas at quarterback, the Colts won a club record 11 consecutive games in 1964, clinching their third Western Conference title. Baltimore made their first Superbowl appearance in 1968, but lost 16-7 to the New York Jets. It wasn't until 1971 in Superbowl V, that the Colts became World Champions, beating the Dallas Cowboys 16-13 on a 32-yard field goal five seconds from the end.

In the strike-shortened 1982 season the Colts finished with a miserable 0-8-1 record, and therefore had first pick in the 1983 NFL draft. They selected Stanford quarterback John Elway but there was no way that Elway would go to Baltimore. He said he would rather play baseball than play football as a Colt. After a lot of horse-trading the Colts allowed Elway to go to Denver in exchange for their 1983 first round choice offensive tackle Chris Hinton along with quarterback Mark Herrmann and Denver's first round choice in the 1983 NFL draft.

The 1983 season was not one the Colts could write home about, 7 wins and 9 losses.

Last season

Widely tipped to be the league's whipping boys, the Colts did

50

Indianapolis Colts vs NFL

	Won	Lost	Tied
Atlanta	8	0	0
Buffalo	15	15	1
Chicago	21	14	0
Cincinnati	5	4	0
Cleveland	5	10	0
Dallas	3	6	0
Denver	1	6	0
Detroit	17	16	2
Green Bay	17	18	1
Houston	5	3	0
Kansas City	3	6	0
Los Angeles Raiders	2	4	0
Los Angeles Rams	20	14	2
Miami	9	24	0
Minnesota	12	5	1
New England	15	16	0
New Orleans	3	0	0
New York Giants	7	3	0
New York Jets	16	16	0
Philadelphia	5	5	0
Pittsburgh	4	9	0
San Diego	2	4	0
San Francisco	21	14	0
St Louis	4	5	0
Seattle	2	0	0
Tampa Bay	2	1	0
Washington	15	6	0

well to finish 5-11. But although they did better than expected, coach Rod Dowhower's team still had a hard struggle. Quarterback Mike Pagel didn't rate as one of the season's most successful players, but then, he didn't receive too much

End-of-season depth chart

OFFENSE

WR   — 85 Matt Bouza, 86 Oliver Williams, 80 Ricky Nichols
OLT   — 75 Chris Hinton, 71 Kevin Call
OLG   — 64 Ben Utt
C   — 53 Ray Donaldson, 61 Don Bailey
ORG   — 74 Roger Caron
ORT   — 72 Karl Baldischwiler, 71 Kevin Call
TE   — 81 Pat Beach, 84 Mark Boyer
WR   — 87 Wayne Capers, 88 Robbie Martin
QB   — 18 Mike Pagel, 12 Matt Kofler
RB   — 32 Randy McMillan, 44 Owen Gill
RB   — 34 George Wonsley, 20 Albert Bentley

DEFENSE

DLE   — 99 Donnell Thompson, 94 Scott Virkus
NT   — 92 Brad White, 68 Willie Broughton
DRE   — 95 Chris Scott, 91 Byron Smith, Charles Benson
LOLB   — 98 Johnie Cooks, 59 Orlando Lowry
LILB   — 93 Cliff Odom, 56 LaMonte Hunley
RILB   — 55 Barry Krauss, 57 Dave Ahrens
ROLB   — 50 Duane Bickett, 59 Orlando Lowry
LCB   — 27 Preston Davis, 42 Keith Lee, 36 Don Anderson
RCB   — 38 Eugene Daniel, 42 Keith Lee, 36 Don Anderson
SS   — 25 Nesby Glasgow, 47 Leonard Coleman
FS   — 37 Anthony Young, 35 Tate Randle

SPECIAL TEAMS

P   — 3 Rohn Stark
K   — 2 Raul Allegre
H   — 3 Rohn Stark
PR   — 88 Robbie Martin, 37 Anthony Young
KR   — 88 Robbie Martin, 20 Albert Bentley
LSN   — 61 Don Bailey, 53 Ray Donaldson

ALSO WITH THE INDIANAPOLIS COLTS
James Harbour (WR), 63 Mark Kirchner (T),
Keli McGregor (TE), 76 Jim Mills (T), 83 Tim Sherwin (TE),
Mark Smith (WR), 66 Ron Solt (G), 96 Blaise Winter (DE),
69 Leo Wisniewski (NT)

protection from his line. Running back George Wonsley carried the rushing game, and British-born Owen Gill looked useful on those occasions when he had a chance to shine. In the air, ex-Steeler Wayne Capers laid some prodigious leaps and had a fine season.

There were no surprises on defense, despite solid and sterling work from Barry Krauss, Cliff Odom and Johnie Cooks. But that just about sums up the Colts' 1985 campaign: solid enough, but you never really noticed that they were there.

Prediction

It's a sad, sad situation up there in Indianapolis. Don't expect post-season action this time around.

Play-off prediction

0

Kansas City Chiefs

AMERICAN FOOTBALL CONFERENCE — WESTERN DIVISION

Address:　　　　　1 Arrowhead Drive, Kansas City, Missouri 64129

Telephone:　　　　(816) 924-9300

Colours:　　　　　Red, gold and white

Stadium:　　　　　Arrowhead Stadium (*address as above*)

Capacity:　　　　　78,067

Playing surface:　　AstroTurf 8

History

The father of the Chiefs, Lamar Hunt, has been one of the most dramatic forces in the development of the game since 1960. It was he who founded and organized the American Football League in six cities: New York, Houston, Denver, Los Angeles, Minneapolis and his own home town Dallas. Without Hunt there would have been no AFL. His Dallas team — the Texans — were an exciting and successful team, winning the AFL Championship against Houston on 21 December 1962.

In 1963 (after an offer from the Mayor of Kansas City to move his team to Missouri) Hunt — knowing that Kansas was football-starved — moved his franchise, and renamed the team the Chiefs. They started their first season well, beating Denver 59-7, but they could only manage one win and two ties in their next nine games. Then in 1964, burdened by injuries, the team played badly and attendances dropped — there was talk that year of the Chiefs folding. But they endured, building up the team under the direction of head coach Hank Stram, and by 1967 the Chiefs became the first AFL team to contest the Superbowl. They faced the mighty Green Bay Packers coached by the legendary Vince Lombardi. The Packers proved that the NFL was the best, whipping the Chiefs 35-10. Despite the fact that the rivalry between the AFL and the NFL was increasing all the time, the crowd for Superbowl I, played at the Los Angeles Memorial Colosseum, was only 61,946 — there were *30,000* empty seats. Even for this very first Superbowl there was hype: in a press conference before the game Fred (The Hammer) Williamson, the Chiefs' defensive back, promised that he would severely punish the Packers because he was going to play rough, and physical. Fine words. Late in the game, it was *he* who was knocked unconscious!

In 1970, the Chiefs saw Superbowl action again, when in Superbowl IV their opponents were the Minnesota Vikings. The Vikings were firm favourites, but with the help of three field goals from kicker Jan Sterenud, the Chiefs became Superbowl Champions 23-7.

The year 1972 saw the opening of their new futuristic Arrowhead Stadium, with a seating capacity of 78,097, which cost a cool $73 million. But the new stadium didn't help the season and they finished 8-6.

In 1975, under a new coach, Paul Wiggin, the Chiefs won four out of five games early in the season, but collapsed as the season wore on and they finished 5-9.

Two years later, Wiggin was fired as the Chiefs lost their first five games. His successor was Tom Bettis, but with six straight losses under his belt Bettis was told his contract was not to be renewed. The Chiefs at last had a winning season in 1981, their first since 1973. After two losing seasons in 1982 and 1983 they managed to go 8 and 8 in 1984.

Last season

The Chiefs started brightly enough, racing to a 3-1 record and dumping the Raiders along the way. But then, just as has happened so often in the past, things started to go wrong, and the Chiefs went into a nosedive from which they could not pull out.

Kansas City Chiefs vs NFL

	Won	Lost	Tied
Atlanta	2	0	0
Buffalo	11	14	1
Chicago	1	2	0
Cincinnati	8	7	0
Cleveland	5	4	1
Dallas	1	2	0
Denver	33	18	0
Detroit	2	2	0
Green Bay	1	1	1
Houston	20	12	0
Indianapolis	6	3	0
Los Angeles Raiders	21	30	2
Los Angeles Rams	0	3	0
Miami	7	6	0
Minnesota	2	2	0
New England	11	7	3
New Orleans	2	2	0
New York Giants	1	4	0
New York Jets	13	11	0
Philadelphia	0	1	0
Pittsburgh	4	9	0
San Diego	24	26	1
San Francisco	1	3	0
St Louis	3	0	1
Seattle	8	7	0
Tampa Bay	3	2	0
Washington	2	1	0

The running game, a Chiefs' weakness for years, couldn't get going, and draftee Ethan Horton failed to live up to his potential. But in the air Stephone Paige set a new NFL record for most yards gained in a single game, and he was ably supported

End-of-season depth chart

OFFENSE

WR	—	88 Carlos Carson, 83 Stephone Paige, 80 George Shorthose
OLT	—	60 Matt Herkenhoff, 70 Billy Shields
OLG	—	77 Rich Baldinger, 65 Rob Fada, 68 Scott Auer
C	—	53 Bob Rush, 62 Adam Lingner
ORG	—	64 Bob Olderman, 68 Scott Auer, 62 Adam Lingner
ORT	—	72 David Lutz, 77 Rich Baldinger
TE	—	87 Walt Arnold, 81 Willie Scott, 85 Jonathan Hayes
WR	—	83 Stephone Paige, 89 Henry Marshall, 82 Anthony Hancock
QB	—	14 Todd Blackledge, 9 Bill Kenney
RB	—	44 Herman Heard, 32 Ethan Horton
RB	—	43 Mike Pruitt, 46 Bruce King

DEFENSE

DLE	—	63 Bill Maas, 74 Pete Koch
NT	—	93 Eric Holle, 63 Bill Maas
DRE	—	71 Dave Lindstrom, 92 Hal Stephens
LOLB	—	50 Calvin Daniels, 52 Ken Jolly
LILB	—	97 Scott Radecic, 57 Jerry Blanton
RILB	—	59 Gary Spani, 57 Jerry Blanton
ROLB	—	52 Ken Jolly, 95 Jeff Paine, 55 Louis Cooper
LCB	—	29 Albert Lewis, 23 Greg Hill
RCB	—	31 Kevin Ross, 41 Garcia Lane
SS	—	34 Lloyd Burruss, 30 Mark Robinson
FS	—	20 Deron Cherry, 22 Sherman Cocroft

SPECIAL TEAMS

P	—	6 Jim Arnold
K	—	8 Nick Lowery
H	—	9 Bill Kenney
PR	—	41 Garcia Lane
KR	—	41 Garcia Lane, 82 Anthony Hancock
LSN	—	62 Adam Lingner, 53 Bob Rush

ALSO WITH THE KANSAS CITY CHIEFS

76 John Alt (T), 99 Mike Bell (DE), 66 Brad Budde (G),
90 Bob Hamm (DE), 94 Ken McAlister (LB),
42 Jeff Smith (RB/KR), 67 Art Still (DE)

by Carlos Carson. Quarterback Bill Kenny is getting a bit long in the tooth now, but he showed again that he is one of the NFL's most accurate passers. Backup Todd Blackledge had a good workout towards the end as Kenny was injured.

Safety Deron Cherry was the only star of a defense which perhaps became disheartened by how much time they had to spend on the field. In a team which contains no glaring weaknesses, it sometimes seemed as if the Chiefs beat themselves.

Prediction

Immediately following last year's disappointing season, John Mackovic sat down to pinpoint some of the team's problem areas, and what could be done to put things right. He has made several key changes in his coaching staff: newcomer Frank Gansz, now assistant head coach, says it all: 'If you can get involved and improve one individual's performance, it starts to spread like wildfire to everybody you work with. And now all of a sudden you're making plans, you're better and you're winning the close games.'

That's the stuff... Let's see if it works in practice.

Play-off prediction

3

Los Angeles Raiders

AMERICAN FOOTBALL CONFERENCE — WESTERN DIVISION

Address:	332 Center Street, El Segundo, California 90245
Telephone:	(213) 322-3451
Colours:	Silver, black
Stadium:	Los Angeles Memorial Colosseum, 3911 South Figueroa Street, Los Angeles, California 90037
Capacity:	92,516
Playing surface:	Grass

History

'What I want is enough time and money to build the Raiders into a professional football team.' So said Al Davis, on taking on the head coach and general manager's job of the Oakland Raiders back in 1963. He had the time — he was given the money — and the Raiders have had a commitment to excellence ever since.

Three years earlier, on 30 January 1960, the city of Oakland had gained an AFL franchise. They had two fine young quarterbacks, Tom Flores and Babe Parilli, and a couple of other solid players, but they had little else and they finished their first season with eight losses and six wins.

A year later, hoping to improve their luck, the Raiders were on the move, to Candlestick Park in San Francisco — but their luck didn't change. They finished that season with the dubious distinction of scoring the fewest points, conceding the most, and winning only two games watched by no more than a handful of fans.

Things began to change in 1963 when Al Davis accepted a three-year contract as the Raiders' head coach and general manager. When he took over the Raiders had won only nine games out of forty-two. But since 1967, when they won the AFL League Championship in their first season in the play-offs, the team who prides itself on 'commitment to excellence' have been in the play-offs fourteen times: they have played in twelve Championship games, have captured twelve Divisional Championships, the AFL Championship, three American Football Conference Championships, and have won three World Championships.

From 1963 to 1984 they were truly the winningest team in professional sport. In 1968 the Raiders played what was later to be known as the '*Heidi* game'. They were playing the New York Jets at Oakland and were behind 32-29. There was one minute five seconds left to play. The game was being televized by NBC but, because they were running late, NBC switched from the game to begin the film *Heidi*. NBC's switchboard was jammed with protests; and the viewers became more incensed when they found out the Raiders had come back to win with two late touchdowns, making the final score 43-32. A year later, in 1969, John Madden became the youngest head coach in pro football at 32 years old and he guided Oakland to the play-offs, though they fell 17-7 in the AFC Championship game to Kansas City.

In 1977, having won the Divisional Championship, Oakland met Minnesota in Superbowl IX, whom they beat convincingly 32-14.

In 1979, after ten years as head coach, John Madden retired, and former Oakland quarterback Tom Flores was named as his successor.

In 1980 Jim Plunkett took over as starting quarterback and in doing so took Oakland to six straight victories, their final record 11 wins, five losses. And in the AFC Wild Card game the Raiders beat Houston 27-7. In the AFC Divisional play-off game the Oakland defense surpassed itself and they beat Cleveland 14-12. The following week, in the AFC Championship game, the Raiders beat the Chargers 34-27 and

Los Angeles Raiders vs NFL

	Won	Lost	Tied
Atlanta	4	1	0
Buffalo	12	11	0
Chicago	3	2	0
Cincinnati	12	4	0
Cleveland	9	1	0
Dallas	2	1	0
Denver	36	14	12
Detroit	3	2	0
Green Bay	4	1	0
Houston	21	10	0
Indianapolis	4	2	0
Kansas City	30	21	2
Los Angeles Rams	4	1	0
Miami	14	3	1
Minnesota	4	1	0
New England	12	12	1
New Orleans	3	0	1
New York Giants	3	0	0
New York Jets	12	11	2
Philadelphia	3	1	0
Pittsburgh	9	6	0
San Diego	33	18	2
San Francisco	3	2	0
St Louis	1	1	0
Seattle	9	9	0
Tampa Bay	2	0	0
Washington	4	1	0

advanced to Superbowl XV. The Raiders intimidated and dominated the Eagles — Superbowl victory was theirs, 27-10.

In May 1982 the Raiders won an important court victory which allowed them to move to the Los Angeles Memorial

End-of-season depth chart

OFFENSE

WR	— 84 Jessie Hester, 21 Cliff Branch
OLT	— 79 Bruce Davis, 74 Shelby Jordan
OLG	— 73 Charley Hannah, 60 Curt Marsh
C	— 72 Don Mosebar, 50 Dave Dalby
ORG	— 65 Mickey Marvin, 60 Curt Marsh
ORT	— 70 Henry Lawrence, 74 Shelby Jordan
TE	— 46 Todd Christensen, 87 Trey Junkin, 81 Andy Parker
WR	— 85 Dokie Williams, 83 Tim Moffett
QB	— 6 Marc Wilson, 12 Rusty Hilger
RB	— 27 Frank Hawkins, 31 Derrick Jensen
RB	— 32 Marcus Allen, 33 Kenny King

DEFENSE

DLE	— 75 Howie Long, 93 Greg Townsend
MG	— 71 Bill Pickel, 98 Mitch Willis
DRE	— 99 Sean Jones, 94 Elvis Franks
LOLB	— 91 Brad Van Pelt, 56 Jeff Barnes
LILB	— 55 Matt Millen, 57 Jerry Robinson
RILB	— 54 Reggie McKenzie, 57 Jerry Robinson
ROLB	— 53 Rod Martin, 58 Jack Squirek
LCB	— 37 Lester Hayes, 43 Sam Seale
RCB	— 22 Mike Haynes, 45 James Davis
SS	— 36 Mike Davis, 30 Stacey Toran, 41 Fulton Walker
FS	— 26 Vann McElroy, 23 Odis McKinney, 41 Fulton Walker

SPECIAL TEAMS

P	— 8 Ray Guy, 10 Chris Bahr
K	— 10 Chris Bahr, 8 Ray Guy
H	— 6 Marc Wilson, 8 Ray Guy, 83 Tim Moffett
PR	— 41 Fulton Walker, 22 Mike Haynes, 83 Tim Moffett
KR	— 43 Sam Seale, 41 Fulton Walker, 33 Kenny King
LSN(P)	— 87 Trey Junkin, 81 Andy Parker
LSN(F)	— 50 Dave Dalby, 73 Charley Hannah

ALSO WITH THE LOS ANGELES RAIDERS
77 Lyle Alzado (DE), 90 Larry McCoy (LB),
28 Cle Montgomery (WR/KR), 51 Bob Nelson (LB),
16 Jim Plunkett (QB), 86 Jim Smith (WR)

Colosseum and on 29 August 1982 they played their first pre-season game, beating the Packers 24-3. The regular season started well for them. They beat the defending Superbowl Champions, the 49ers, 23-17. LA fans liked having the silver and black around and on 18 December 1982 they recorded the first million-dollar home game in NFL history when they beat their neighbours and old rivals the Rams 37-31.

On 1 January 1984, before the largest Championship crowd in AFC history (92,335), the Raiders beat the Seahawks 30-14 and went to meet the Washington Redskins in Superbowl XVIII at Tampa Bay. Before a TV and radio audience of over 125 million and in front of a crowd of 72,000, they flattened the Redskins 38-9. Tinseltown went wild. The World Champion Raiders were given the key to the city of LA.

On 9 December 1984 the Raiders saw play-off action for the fourteenth time in eighteen years but in the AFC Wild Card play-off game on 22 December they lost 13-7 to Seattle.

Last season

The Raiders managed to lift the AFC West pennant last year against all the odds, a tribute indeed to the coaching genius of Tom Flores. But you need a good quarterback to progress further, and that's where the Raiders fall down. In the absence of ageing and injury-plagued Jim Plunkett, Mark Wilson finally had his chance, and he couldn't live up to what was expected. In the play-off game against New England, Wilson was constantly booed by the Raider fans. The Raiders again concentrated on the running ability of 'Rocket Man' Marcus Allen, who ran for nine consecutive hundred-yard games, and all credit should go to tight end Todd Christensen, a man of remarkable agility. This man with the superglue fingers caught everything that was flung at him.

A rebuilt defense hit it off immediately, with new boys such as Reggie McKenzie blending in with old stagers such as Howie Long and Rod Martin. The Raiders are the NFL's mean machine on defense, and they proved it again last year.

Prediction

You don't win Superbowls with suspect quarterbacks. Perhaps Wilson will shine this year. If he does then the Raiders could go all the way.

Play-off prediction

9

Miami Dolphins

AMERICAN FOOTBALL CONFERENCE — EASTERN DIVISION

Address:	4770 Biscayne Boulevard, Suite 1440, Miami, Florida 33137
Telephone:	(305) 576-1000
Colours:	Aqua, coral and white
Stadium:	Orange Bowl, 1501 N.W. Third Street, Miami, Florida 33125
Capacity:	75,206
Playing surface:	Grass

History

It cost $7,500,000 back in 1965 to start an AFL franchise in the rapidly growing market in Miami, and we owe the name to Mrs Robert Swanson of West Miami, whose suggestion of naming the team 'the Dolphins' was chosen from over 20,000 entries. 'The dolphin is one of the fastest and smartest creatures of the sea. Dolphins can attack and kill a whale or a shark. Sailors say bad luck will come to anyone who harms a dolphin.' So said Joseph Robbie on 8 October 1965 when the Dolphins were named.

Joseph Robbie, a lawyer from Minneapolis, was the one who paid the $7,500,000 — but it was not all plain sailing in those early days. On 16 October 1966 the Dolphins ended a string of nine losses by beating Denver 24-7, but it was taking the good citizens of Miami some time to come to terms with their newly-formed Dolphins. Only 23,000 people turned up to see their first win.

Things started happening in 1967 in the first round of the AFL/NFL draft. Miami drafted a young quarterback called Bob Griese. They gave him the number 12 shirt and as owner Joseph Robbi commented 'Number twelve is the cornerstone of this franchise'. Griese finished his first season fifth among NFL passers.

But it was in 1970 that the modern Dolphins were formed, when 40-year-old Don Shula left Baltimore to become head coach. Shula was, and still is, a strict disciplinarian, and put the Dolphins through a torturing training camp the like of which they had never seen before. At 7 a.m. every morning they would start with a two-mile run, followed by two 90-minute practices, followed by a walk-through. This gruelling schedule day after day paid off, and they won their first five League games.

In 1972 they reached their first Superbowl, but lost to Dallas 24-3. 'We'll be back,' vowed owner Robbie, and of course they were.

The next season became a landmark in NFL history, as the Dolphins played the entire season without losing a game. They sailed through the play-offs, and it became the perfect season when in Superbowl VII they defeated the Redskins 14-7.

In 1974, they were back in the Superbowl and beat Minnesota 24-7, and thus became only the second team ever to win two consecutive Superbowls.

In 1975-76 the Dolphins became mortals again. Baltimore knocked them out of the play-offs for the first time since 1970. And in 1976 Don Shula suffered his first losing season in 14 years as head coach with a lowly 6-8 record.

In 1978 Bob Griese suffered torn ligaments in his left knee and Don Strock took over at quarterback. His best game was against Baltimore when he threw for three touchdowns.

In 1983, for the first time in nine years, the Dolphins won a play-off game beating the Patriots 28-13 and by beating the San Diego Chargers — and the New York Jets — they won the AFC title. In a thrilling Superbowl contest against the Washington Redskins on 30 January, despite leading with only ten minutes remaining, they lost 27-17.

On 26 April 1983, for the first time in Dolphin history, they

Miami Dolphins vs NFL

	Won	Lost	Tied
Atlanta	4	0	0
Buffalo	32	7	1
Chicago	4	0	0
Cincinnati	7	3	0
Cleveland	3	3	0
Dallas	3	2	0
Denver	5	2	1
Detroit	2	1	0
Green Bay	4	0	0
Houston	9	10	0
Indianapolis	24	9	0
Kansas City	6	7	0
Los Angeles Raiders	3	14	1
Los Angeles Rams	3	1	0
Minnesota	4	1	0
New England	25	15	0
New Orleans	3	1	0
New York Giants	1	0	0
New York Jets	22	18	1
Philadelphia	3	2	0
Pittsburgh	7	3	0
San Diego	5	8	0
San Francisco	4	1	0
St Louis	5	0	0
Seattle	3	1	0
Tampa Bay	2	1	0
Washington	4	2	0

drafted a quarterback. His name... Dan Marino. But despite this gifted young man, the Dolphins lost their Conference semifinal game 27-20 to the Seattle Seahawks.

In 1984, Miami ended the regular season with the best record

End-of-season depth chart

OFFENSE

WR	—	85 Mark Duper, 89 Nat Moore, 11 Jim Jensen
OLT	—	79 Jon Giesler, 65 Jeff Dellenbach
OLG	—	61 Roy Foster, 63 Larry Lee
C	—	57 Dwight Stephenson, 63 Larry Lee, 76 Steve Clark
ORG	—	76 Steve Clark, 63 Larry Lee
ORT	—	74 Cleveland Green, 72 Ronnie Lee
TE	—	84 Bruce Hardy, 87 Dan Johnson, 80 Joe Rose
WR	—	83 Mark Clayton, 32 Tom Vigorito, 11 Jim Jensen
QB	—	13 Dan Marino, 10 Don Strock, 11 Jim Jensen
RB	—	22 Tony Nathan, 27 Lorenzo Hampton, 23 Joe Carter
RB	—	34 Woody Bennett, 30 Ron Davenport

DEFENSE

DLE	—	75 Doug Betters, 91 Mack Moore
NT	—	71 Mike Charles, 99 George Little, 70 Bill Barnett
DRE	—	58 Kim Bokamper, 71 Mike Charles, 99 George Little
LOLB	—	59 Bob Brudzinski, 54 Alex Moyer
LILB	—	53 Jay Brophy, 50 Jackie Shipp
RILB	—	51 Mark Brown, 50 Jackie Shipp
ROLB	—	55 Hugh Green, 52 Robin Sendlein
LCB	—	44 Paul Lankford, 28 Don McNeal
RCB	—	49 William Judson, 18 Mike Smith
SS	—	47 Glenn Blackwood, 42 Lyle Blackwood
FS	—	42 Bud Brown, 42 Lyle Blackwood

SPECIAL TEAMS

P	—	4 Reggie Roby, 10 Don Strock
K	—	7 Fuad Reveiz, 4 Reggie Roby
H	—	10 Don Strock, 11 Jim Jensen
PR	—	32 Tom Vigorito, 83 Mark Clayton, 23 Joe Carter
KR	—	27 Lorenzo Hampton, 23 Joe Carter
LSN(P)	—	84 Bruce Hardy, 76 Steve Clark
LSN(F)	—	63 Larry Lee, 76 Steve Clark, 74 Cleveland Green

ALSO WITH THE MIAMI DOLPHINS
73 Bob Baumhower (NT), 56 Charles Bowser (LB),
24 Duan Hanks (WR), 88 Vince Heflin (WR),
40 Mike Kozlowski (S), 64 Ed Newman (G),
9 Joe Pisarcik (QB), 45 Robert Sowell (CB), 60 Jeff Toews (G)

in the AFC, 14-2; Marino became the first-ever NFL quarterback to pass for over 5,000 yards. Both Mark Clayton and Mark Duper set new Dolphin records for receptions and reception yardage. So Superbowl-bound again. But Superbowl XIX was a bitter disappointment for Shula and his Dolphins. In front of 84,059 fans in Stanford Stadium in Palo Alto California, and millions around the world, the Dolphins fell 38-16 to the vastly superior San Francisco 49ers.

Last season

Despite a slow start (a loss to Houston and a struggle over Indianapolis), the Dolphins got back into the groove once again. Quarterback Dan Marino found his feet after a summer holdout. He is still the fastest and the best in the game today — only Dan Fouts of San Diego throws more often.

The running game was a bit one-paced again (a perennial fault), but the rookie running back Ron Davenport made a name for himself in short yardage situations. In overall terms it was a good year for Dolphin new boys. Injuries and retirements left a few gaps on defense, and rookie kicker Fuad Reveiz was a revelation.

But despite the free-scoring nature of the offense (Dan Marino picked Chicago apart at will), Miami has one of the weaker defensive units, especially against the run. In the play-off game in Cleveland, for example, it was humidity, not Dolphin tackles, which slowed Mack and Byner.

Prediction

The old adage is that defense wins Superbowls, and coach Shula will have to strengthen that area if he is to add another Superbowl Ring to his collection. Marino and the rest of the offense can be spectacularly good, and last year's contract holdout by this gifted young quarterback did a great deal of damage. This time around there shouldn't .be the same problems. Put some money on Miami now!

Play-off prediction

10

New England Patriots

AMERICAN FOOTBALL CONFERENCE — EASTERN DIVISION

Address: Sullivan Stadium, Route 1, Foxboro, Massachusetts 02035

Telephone: (617) 543-7911 or 262-1776

Colours: Red, white and blue

Stadium: Sullivan Stadium (*address as above*)

Playing surface: Super Turf

History

It was in 1959 that the American Football League's eighth franchise was given to Boston, but it was a shaky start financially — the team lost nearly $350,000 in its first season. Despite the loss, Boston liked having the Patriots around — they had been football-starved for eleven years — but it was not until 1963 when they tied for first place in their division with a 7-6-1 record that things began to change. Despite being killed by the San Diego Chargers 51-10, the Patriots announced that for the first time in their history they had finished the season in profit, and as they were the first major-league, professional sports team to issue public stock, this was a real milestone.

In 1970, the Patriots changed homes. Foxboro was to become the team's home ground, and in 1971 because they were moving out of the Boston area, they changed their name from the Boston Patriots to the New England Patriots. It was in this year that the Heisman Trophy winner, Jim Plunkett, was drafted; and in his first season he had a very rough ride. The Patriots' offensive line was very leaky and with little protection Plunkett suffered severe punishment.

73

For three miserable seasons, injury followed injury for the hapless Plunkett, and so did controversy. Plunkett's eventual replacement during this injury-prone period was Steve Grogan, and the talk in the locker rooms of the players and the living rooms of the fans was a 'who's better, Plunkett or Grogan' debate.

The controversy didn't last that long, because in 1976 in a significant draft Plunkett was sent to San Francisco. With Grogan at the controls the Patriots at last had a spring in their stride. After a shaky start, Grogan guided them to a Wild Card spot in the AFC play-offs, meeting the Oakland Raiders. It was a close-run thing — the Patriots lost 24-21, when the Raiders scored with 39 seconds left on the clock.

The year 1981 saw the Patriots' worst season, winning only two of 16 games. Their coach Ron Erhardt was fired and was replaced by Ron Meyer.

On 8 January 1983 in their first play-off game since 1978, the Patriots lost to the eventual AFC Champions, the Miami Dolphins 28-13. On 29 June Shaeffer Stadium was officially renamed Sullivan Stadium in honour of the Patriots' owner 'Billy' Sullivan. On 25 October 1984 Raymond Berry was named head coach, replacing Ron Meyer, and three days later in celebrating the team's 25th anniversary, they beat the New York Jets 30-20. It was a good season for second year quarterback Tony Eason who established a new one-season pass completion record of 236.

Last season

If it were possible to talk about the Patriots up until the moment they took the field against Chicago, you would say that theirs was one of the most remarkable success stories of the year. But the humiliation at the hands of the Bears, and the subsequent drugs revelations, have left a sour taste in the mouth. The quietly determined coaching of Raymond Berry brought out the best in running back Craig James, who rushed his way to the Pro Bowl along with offensive lineman Brian Holloway and John Hannah. And while the passing game wasn't always reliable (allowing for Irving Fryar's flashes of brilliance), quarterbacks Tony Eason and Steve Grogan had plenty of

74

New England Patriots vs NFL

	Won	Lost	Tied
Atlanta	2	2	0
Buffalo	28	23	1
Chicago	2	3	0
Cincinnati	6	3	0
Cleveland	2	6	0
Dallas	0	5	0
Denver	12	11	0
Detroit	2	2	0
Green Bay	2	1	0
Houston	14	13	1
Indianapolis	16	15	0
Kansas City	7	11	3
Los Angeles Raiders	12	12	1
Los Angeles Rams	2	1	0
Miami	15	25	0
Minnesota	2	1	0
New Orleans	4	0	0
New York Giants	1	1	0
New York Jets	21	29	1
Philadelphia	2	3	0
Pittsburgh	2	5	0
San Diego	13	12	2
San Francisco	1	3	0
St Louis	1	4	0
Seattle	5	1	0
Tampa Bay	2	0	0
Washington	1	3	0

options.

The opportunistic defense forced mistakes and capitalized on them. The linebacking crew of Andre Tippett and Don Blackmon were especially rugged, while a secondary which

End-of-season depth chart

OFFENSE

WR	—	85 Stanley Morgan, 83 Cedric Jones
OLT	—	76 Brian Holloway, 70 Art Plunkett, 67 Steve Moore
OLG	—	73 John Hannah, 75 Guy Morriss
C	—	58 Pete Brock, 75 Guy Morriss
ORG	—	61 Ron Wooten, 66 Paul Fairchild
ORT	—	67 Steve Moore, 70 Art Plunkett
TE	—	87 Lin Dawson, 88 Derrick Ramsey
WR	—	80 Irving Fryar, 81 Stephen Starring, 27 Greg Hawthorne
QB	—	11 Tony Eason, 14 Steve Grogan, 12 Tom Ramsey
RB	—	32 Craig James, 30 Mosi Tatupu
RB	—	33 Tony Collins, 24 Robert Weathers

DEFENSE

DLE	—	60 Garin Veris, 92 Smiley Creswell
NT	—	72 Lester Williams, 98 Dennis Owens
DRE	—	85 Julius Adams, 99 Ben Thomas
LOLB	—	56 Andre Tippett, 54 Ed Williams
LILB	—	57 Steve Nelson, 95 Ed Reynolds
RILB	—	50 Larry McGrew, 52 Johnny Rembert
ROLB	—	55 Don Blackmon, 51 Brian Ingram
LCB	—	42 Ronnie Lippett, 23 Rod McSwain
RCB	—	26 Raymond Clayborn, 43 Ernest Gibson
SS	—	38 Roland James, 28 Jim Bowman
FS	—	31 Fred Marion, 28 Jim Bowman

SPECIAL TEAMS

P	—	3 Rich Camarillo, 1 Tony Franklin
K	—	1 Tony Franklin, 3 Rich Camarillo
H	—	11 Tony Eason, 12 Tom Ramsey
PR	—	80 Irving Fryar, 38 Roland James, 31 Fred Marion
KR	—	81 Stephen Starring, 80 Irving Fryar 83 Cedric Jones
LSN	—	75 Guy Morriss, 61 Ron Wooten, 52 Johnny Rembert

ALSO WITH THE NEW ENGLAND PATRIOTS
68 Darryl Haley (T), 64 Trevor Matich (C),
41 Bo Robinson (RB), 77 Kenneth Sims (DE),
53 Clayton Weishuhn (LB), Derwin Williams (WR),
44 Jon Williams (RB), 90 Toby Williams (DE)

listed such predators as Fred Marion and Ronnie Lippett was always capable of coming up with big play. Let's hope they all recovered from the Superbowl disaster.

Prediction

Cynics have been heard to say that despite their opportunistic play of last year the Patriots are not the best team in the AFC. They're bound to make the play-offs again this year *if* the defense remains solid, *if* they stay healthy, and *if* they stay lucky. This time round, their schedule is going to be more difficult, but they — along with the Bears, of course — are going to be the team to beat. We live in interesting times!

Play-off prediction

7

New York Jets

AMERICAN FOOTBALL CONFERENCE — EASTERN DIVISION

Address:	598 Madison Avenue, New York, New York 10022
Telephone:	(212) 421-6600
Colours:	'Kelly' green and white
Stadium:	Giants Stadium, East Rutherford, New Jersey 07073
Capacity:	76,891
Playing surface:	AstroTurf

History

They were originally called the Titans when a franchise was given to New York on 14 August 1959, and they immediately signed the Washington Redskins' top-rated passer Sammy Baugh as their first coach. He didn't leave Washington for peanuts either, his starting salary was $28,000 — a fortune in 1959. The Titans' colours at that time were blue and gold (the familiar green came later) but they needed to be seen by a wider audience. Their owner, Harry Wismer, was an astute businessman and signed a five-year deal to have AFL games televised. Their first-year fee from television was $1,785,000 and in their first League game they came out and beat Buffalo 27-3.

Despite this, New Yorkers seemed uninterested in the Titans. In 1972, in seven home games a mere 36,000 people went to watch the Titans. The club was near bankrupt and in 1963, after a coaching conflict and with financial trouble mounting, a five-man syndicate purchased the New York franchise for $1 million, and on that day — 28 March — the Titans became the Jets.

In 1964 the Jets made the most significant trade in the history of the franchise, and on the entire AFL. They wanted a number one draft choice, and after some horse-trading they got what they wanted — and more than they bargained for. They chose a man from Alabama called Joe Namath. His initial salary was reported to be worth $427,000. Before he became a Jet, Namath had to undergo surgery on his right knee (an injury sustained while playing for Alabama), and he started for the Jets on 18 September 1965. He immediately showed his brilliance, and passed for 287 yards, fininishing the season as the AFL Rookie of the Year, throwing 18 touchdowns and gaining 2,220 yards.

In 1967, Namath was going from strength to strength and finished the season with 4,007 yards passing, the only pro quarterback to achieve that many yards. With Namath at the helm, the Jets sold out all their home games.

In 1969, Namath (whilst talking to the press) after the Jets' AFL Championship win over the Raiders, personally guaranteed that the Jets would beat Baltimore in Superbowl III. Namath's guarantee made all the headlines — and made him a legend, when New York did indeed beat Buffalo 16-7, and thus became the first AFL team ever to win a Superbowl.

The year 1971 saw join the Jets another young man who was also destined to become a legend — John Riggins. All was not well with Namath, his injured knee needed surgery again and again, and in the season that Riggins joined, Namath was off for three and a half months. However, in 1972 he signed a contract that made him the highest-paid player in the game. Namath received $250,000 a year. The money did wonders: in the best day of his career Namath passed for 496 yards and 6 touchdowns to defeat Baltimore. John Riggins was no slouch either. He ran for 168 yards.

There was a bad start to 1974. After losing seven of their first eight games, the Jets met the Giants at Yale Bowl, and in what turned out to be an emotional game, the Jets snatched victory in overtime 26-20. They then won six in a row.

The Jets had a disastrous season in 1975, finishing with a 2-7 record, but John Riggins was showing his greatness, becoming

New York Jets vs NFL

	Won	Lost	Tied
Atlanta	1	2	0
Buffalo	25	26	0
Chicago	1	2	0
Cincinnati	7	3	0
Cleveland	3	7	0
Dallas	0	3	0
Denver	10	10	1
Detroit	2	2	0
Green Bay	4	1	0
Houston	10	15	1
Indianapolis	16	16	0
Kansas City	10	13	0
Los Angeles Raiders	11	12	2
Los Angeles Rams	2	2	0
Miami	18	22	1
Minnesota	3	1	0
New England	29	22	1
New Orleans	3	1	0
New York Giants	2	2	0
Philadelphia	0	3	0
Pittsburgh	0	8	0
San Diego	7	14	1
San Francisco	1	3	0
St Louis	1	2	0
Seattle	1	7	0
Tampa Bay	3	1	0
Washington	0	3	0

the first Jet to gain over 1,000 yards.

Namath wanted to leave the Jets and on 12 May 1977 signed as a free agent with the Rams — but eight months later he announced his retirement from pro football.

End-of-season depth chart

OFFENSE

WR	—	88 Al Toon, 85 Wesley Walker, 84 Bobby Humphery
OLT	—	68 Reggie McElroy, 64 Guy Bingham
OLG	—	53 Jim Sweeney, 64 Guy Bingham
C	—	65 Joe Fields, 64 Guy Bingham, 61 Greg Gunter
ORG	—	60 Dan Alexander, 64 Guy Bingham
ORT	—	79 Marvin Powell, 64 Guy Bingham
TE	—	82 Mickey Shuler, 89 Rocky Klever, 81 Billy Griggs
WR	—	85 Wesley Walker, 87 Kurt Sohn, 83 JoJo Townsell
QB	—	7 Ken O'Brien, 10 Pat Ryan
RB	—	24 Freeman McNeil, 34 Johnny Hector
RB	—	49 Tony Paige, 23 Dennis Bilgen

DEFENSE

DLE	—	99 Mark Gastineau, 93 Marty Lyons, 76 Ben Rudolph
NT	—	73 Joe Klecko, 95 Tom Baldwin
DRE	—	78 Barry Bennett, 99 Mark Gastineau, 76 Ben Rudolph
LOLB	—	55 Charles Jackson, 50 Bob Crable
LILB	—	59 Kyle Clifton, 58 Matt Monger
RILB	—	56 Lance Mehl, 58 Matt Monger, 57 John Woodring
ROLB	—	50 Bob Crable, 58 Matt Monger
LCB	—	27 Russell Carter, 20 Davlin Mullen
RCB	—	29 Johnny Lynn, 35 Kerry Glenn, Carl Howard
SS	—	21 Kirk Springs, 26 Lester Lyles, Larry Flowers
FS	—	39 Harry Hamilton, 29 Johnny Lynn, 36 Rich Miano

SPECIAL TEAMS

P	—	13 Dave Jennings
K	—	5 Pat Leahy
H	—	10 Pat Ryan, 7 Ken O'Brien
PR	—	21 Kirk Springs, 20 Davlin Mullen
KR	—	34 Johnny Hector, 84 Bobby Humphery
LSN	—	64 Guy Bingham, 65 Joe Fields

ALSO WITH THE NEW YORK JETS
63 Ted Banker (T/G), 31 Marion Barber (RB),
54 Troy Benson (LB), Scott Collins (LB), 86 Glenn Dennison (TE),
37 Donnie Elder (CB), 94 Rusty Guilbeau (LB),
40 Bobby Jackson (CB), 70 Stan Waldemore (G/T),
80 Johnny 'Lam' Jones (WR), Brian Luft (T)

In 1981 the Jets qualified for a Wild Card game, and this is when their defense, led by Joe Klecko and Mark Gastineau, became known as the New York sack exchange. In that season they notched up 66 sacks. Unfortunately for the Jets, the exchange was closed for the Wild Card game, as the Bills won 31-27.

In 1983 as Freeman McNeill became the first Jet to lead the NFL in rushing, the Jets advanced to the Championship game in a rain-sodden Orangebowl Miami. It was a disaster. The Jets were shut out 14-0, and it was that year that the Jets announced they would be moving to the Meadowlands for the 1984 season. 'Shea Stadium is run down and neglected, and the NFL's poorest facility for athletes and spectators alike.' Despite pleas from the Mayor of New York, the Jets left Shea Stadium and made their new home alongside the Giants in East Rutherford, New Jersey.

In their first year at Giants Stadium, under coach Joe Walton, the Jets finished third in the AFC East, notching up seven wins and nine losses.

Last season

With quarterback Ken O'Brien firmly at the helm, running back Freeman McNeil making the most of some tremendous blocking on the ground, and rookie wideout Al Toon drawing gasps of amazement from Jets' fans, it looked as if the New York outfit could score at will (they did against Tampa Bay, racking up 62 points).

The restructured 3-4 defense, in which the line of Mark Gastineau, Joe Klecko and Barry Bennett was outstanding, was inspired by the performances of linebacker Lance Mehl. But an injury-ravaged secondary spoilt things for coach Walton.

In overall terms, the Jets at last showed glimpses of their true potential, but there are a few doubts about Walton. Is he just a little *too* predictable?

Prediction

They were so close last year, second in the AFC East to Miami with a record of 11 and 5 (the same as the Patriots). The Jets could well be flying again this year. They have all the components they need, Walton has to put them all together. The Jets have the potential to go all the way to Pasadena this time round.

Play-off prediction

9

Pittsburg Steelers

AMERICAN FOOTBALL CONFERENCE — CENTRAL DIVISION

Address: Three Rivers Stadium, 300 Stadium Circle, Pittsburgh, Pennsylvania 15212

Telephone: (412) 323-1200

Colours: Black and gold

Stadium: Three Rivers Stadium (*address as above*)

Capacity: 59,000

Playing surface: AstroTurf

History

A 32-year-old ex-boxer called Art Rooney purchased an NFL franchise for Pittsburgh in 1933 — the cost $2,500. But owning the Pittsburgh Pirates was not a lot of fun for Rooney, who saw his club compile 24 wins, 62 losses and 5 ties from 1933 to 1940. Rooney called it a day and sold out, and the Pirates became the Steelers.

The 1950s and 60s saw some success, though the Steelers never made the play-offs. But it was the 1970s that belonged to the Steelers, as pro football's most successful team. They won four Superbowls — making the play-offs eight consecutive times — a dynasty indeed.

The key to this success was their coach, Chuck Noll, who by astute use of the draft built a team of astonishing quality. They had a great defense built around 'Mean' Joe Green, and in 1970 their offense became explosive, with the drafting of quarterback Terry Bradshaw. If Bradshaw needed a perfect foil, he came in the shape of 230-lb (16 stone 6 lb) 6 ft 2 in rookie fullback, Franco Harris. In 1972 when he was named Rookie of the Year he rushed for 1,055 yards, caught 21 passes, and scored 11 touchdowns.

In 1972 the Steelers captured their first Divisional title in their 40-year history. And it was that year that Franco Harris did something miraculous.

It was the 1972 American Conference Divisional play-off, Pittsburgh against Oakland — there were 22 seconds left on the clock, and the Steelers were down 7-6, they were on a fourth down and ten on their own 40-yard line. Although Bradshaw had thrown incompletions on three consecutive attempts, he decided to throw one final time. He aimed for his running back 'Frenchie' Fuqua — the ball missed Fuqua, deflected off Oakland's Jack Tatum and in full stride Harris caught the ball and made the touchdown. 'He was hustling, and good things happen to people who hustle,' Chuck Noll said afterwards, as he and the Steelers celebrated the final score, Pittsburgh 13 Oakland 7. The incident became known as the 'immaculate reception'.

Despite winning their first Divisional title, they lost to the eventual NFL Champions Miami in the AFC Championship game.

In 1974, they won the AFC Central Division title in a 21-17 win against New England, and in the AFC Championship game Pittsburgh's famed steel curtain defense was brilliant — conceding 29 yards rushing and with Franco Harris rushing for 111 yards and two touchdowns, the Steelers beat the Raiders 24-13. They went on to meet Minnesota in Superbowl IX, and won hands down 16-6, with Harris setting a new Superbowl record of 158 yards.

In 1975 the Steelers won the AFC Championship 16-10 over their old foes the Raiders — so Superbowl X beckoned. Their opponents, the Dallas Cowboys, fell to the Steelers 21-17, and the Steelers became the third team ever to win consecutive Superbowls.

In 1979 they were the first team to win three Superbowls when they beat Dallas in Superbowl XIII, and by defeating the Rams the following year in Superbowl XIV, they became the first team to win four Superbowls and win two consecutively. Their

Pittsburgh Steelers vs NFL

	Won	Lost	Tied
Atlanta	6	1	0
Buffalo	6	3	0
Chicago	4	13	1
Cincinnati	17	14	0
Cleveland	31	41	0
Dallas	12	11	0
Denver	5	7	1
Detroit	8	13	1
Green Bay	10	16	0
Houston	24	9	0
Indianapolis	9	4	0
Kansas City	9	4	0
Los Angeles Raiders	6	9	0
Los Angeles Rams	4	12	2
Miami	3	7	0
Minnesota	4	5	0
New England	5	2	0
New Orleans	4	4	0
New York Giants	26	41	3
New York Jets	8	0	0
Philadelphia	25	42	3
San Diego	8	4	0
San Francisco	6	6	0
St Louis	29	20	3
Seattle	3	2	0
Tampa Bay	3	0	0
Washington	27	40	3

total of four league Championships is third to Green Bay and Chicago.

As the 1980s started, their eight-year play-off streak ended — no post-season play in 1980 and 1981, but in 1982-83, and 1984

End-of-season depth chart

OFFENSE

WR	—	82 John Stallworth, 85 Calvin Sweeney, 80 Frank Pokorny
OLT	—	65 Ray Pinney, 63 Pete Rostosky
OLG	—	73 Craig Wolfley, 71 Emil Boures
C	—	52 Mike Webster, 60 Randy Rasmussen, 71 Emil Boures
ORG	—	74 Terry Long, 71 Emil Boures, 60 Randy Rasmussen
ORT	—	62 Tunch Ilkin, 63 Pete Rostosky
TE	—	89 Bennie Cunningham, 86 Preston Gothard
WR	—	83 Louis Lipps, 87 Weegie Thompson
QB	—	16 Mark Malone, 19 David Woodley, 10 Scott Campbell
RB	—	34 Walter Abercrombie, 24 Rich Erenberg, 36 Todd Spencer
RB	—	30 Frank Pollard, 47 Steve Morse, 36 Todd Spencer

DEFENSE

DLE	—	93 Keith Willis, 95 John Goodman, 99 Darryl Sims
NT	—	67 Gary Dunn, 95 John Goodman, 78 Mark Catano
DRE	—	92 Keith Gary, 99 Darryl Sims, 95 John Goodman
LOLB	—	57 Mike Merriweather, 91 Gregg Carr, 54 Fred Small
LILB	—	50 David Little, 55 Dennis Winston
RILB	—	56 Robin Cole, 54 Fred Small
ROLB	—	53 Bryan Hinkle, 91 Gregg Carr, 54 Fred Small
LCB	—	49 Dwayne Woodruff, 22 Rick Woods
RCB	—	33 Harvey Clayton, 26 John Swain
SS	—	31 Donnie Shell, 25 Anthony Tuggle
FS	—	21 Eric Williams, 22 Rick Woods, 25 Anthony Tuggle

SPECIAL TEAMS

P	—	18 Harry Newsome
K	—	1 Gary Anderson
H	—	10 Scott Campbell, 18 Harry Newsome
PR	—	83 Louis Lipps, 22 Rick Woods
KR	—	36 Todd Spencer, 24 Rich Erenberg
LSN(P)	—	60 Randy Rasmussen, 65 Ray Pinney
LSN(F)	—	52 Mike Webster, 65 Ray Pinney

ALSO WITH THE PITTSBURGH STEELERS
23 Chris Brown (CB), 42 Dave Edwards (S), 51 Dan Turk (C),
64 Edmund Nelson (DE), 90 Bob Kohrs (LB)

they went to the play-offs. Bradshaw retired in 1983 as the Steelers' all-time leading passer, and Franco Harris retired the same year as the Steelers' all-time leading rusher with 11,950 yards and 91 touchdowns.

Last season

The sloppy Steelers finished 7-9, posting their first losing record since 1971. Most of the team's problems can be traced to the offense, and to quarterbacks in particular. Since Terry Bradshaw retired, no one player has really earned the right to be called his successor. The best prospect, Mark Malone, spent too much time on the sidelines through injury, but there is promise there. Running backs Frank Pollard and Walter Abercrombie are a useful, though not unstoppable tandem, while Louis Lipps and old man John Stalworth make a devastating receiving duo.

Still rugged on defense, the Steelers' linebackers seem to hate even themselves. Robin Cole and Mike Merriweather shine here, while in the secondary ageless safety Donny Shell once again maintained some cohesion in the unit. But coach Chuck Noll knows that the magic seems to have gone, and 1985 will be a year Pittsburgh will want to forget.

Prediction

It's that offense that's the problem. Malone does have potential, but he will need time to gain his confidence. As much as I'd like to, I can't see the Steelers playing post-season this time around.

Play-off prediction

4

San Diego Chargers

AMERICAN FOOTBALL CONFERENCE — WESTERN DIVISION

Address:	San Diego Jack Murphy Stadium, PO Box 20666, San Diego, California 92120
Telephone:	(619) 280-2111
Colours:	Blue, gold and white
Stadium:	San Diego Jack Murphy Stadium (*address as above*)
Capacity:	60,100
Playing surface:	Grass

History

When you stay in a Hilton hotel, don't just be grateful (or not) for the service, be grateful that hotel magnate Barron Hilton formed the original Chargers back in 1959, and spare a thought for a Gerald Courtney of Hollywood who won an expenses-paid holiday to Acapulco. What did Mr Courtney do to win such a prize? He won the contest to name the team. Once the Chargers were named they needed uniforms. And who was the player who first modelled the Chargers' outfits of blue and gold and lightning bolts? None other than a man who is now being groomed for the next Presidency of the United States, Senator Jack Kemp.

In their opening league game in 1960 before a handful of people in the LA Memorial Colosseum, they beat Dallas 21-20. Even fewer people saw them win the AFL Western Division title, overcoming Denver 41-33.

91

It was in 1961 that the AFL allowed Hilton to move to San Diego. And in August that year, in 93° heat, they beat Houston 27-14.

In 1964 they won the AFL Championship, thrashing Boston 51-10. In 1969 they moved their training camp to the University of California, around 90 miles north of San Diego. Their first two games on the road were losses, but when they came home they were greeted by a record crowd of 54,000 in the San Diego Stadium to see them play the New York Jets. The main attraction was, of course, Joe Namath. In a surprisingly close-fought game, the Chargers won 34-27.

The season of 1972 was awful; the Chargers lost eight of their last 10 games and finished bottom of the AFC Western Division. So in 1973, in what some saw as a desperate move, they acquired the legendary but fading Johnnie Unitas at quarterback. Sadly, a back injury benched him for most of the season, and it was then that the rookie quarterback called Dan Fouts took over.

The following year, Unitas announced his intention of retiring.

It was in 1969 that the Chargers drafted Kellen Winslow, and they gained the AFC West Championship with a 12-4 record, their best since 1963. A year later the Chargers won their second consecutive AFC West crown, with a passing attack led by Fouts, who along with Winslow was breaking records with amazing regularity.

Their most exciting game was probably on 2 January 1982, when they met the Dolphins. The Chargers were in front 24-0 in the first quarter — then were losing 38-31 in the fourth. They tied the score with 60 seconds remaining, and after 13 minutes of overtime Rolf Benirschke's 29-yard field goal won the day. But a week later the victory in the AFL Championship was to elude them, when they were thrashed by the Bengals 27-7, in weather as cold as anyone could want: it was 9° below zero, but the wind chill made the temperature drop to an almost incredible – 59°.

In 1964 wide receiver Charlie Joiner set an NFL record with his 650th pass reception and the Mayor of San Diego proudly proclaimed 11 December 'Charlie Joiner Day'. Not many footballers receive such an honour!

San Diego Chargers vs NFL

	Won	Lost	Tied
Atlanta	0	2	0
Buffalo	17	9	2
Chicago	4	1	0
Cincinnati	10	7	0
Cleveland	5	4	1
Dallas	1	2	0
Denver	27	24	1
Detroit	2	3	0
Green Bay	1	3	0
Houston	16	12	1
Indianapolis	4	2	0
Kansas City	26	24	1
Los Angeles Raiders	18	33	2
Los Angeles Rams	1	2	0
Miami	8	5	0
Minnesota	3	3	0
New England	12	13	2
New Orleans	3	0	0
New York Giants	2	2	0
New York Jets	14	7	1
Philadelphia	2	1	0
Pittsburgh	4	8	0
San Francisco	3	1	0
St Louis	2	1	0
Seattle	9	6	0
Tampa Bay	2	0	0
Washington	0	3	0

Last season

It was an all too predictable script for Chargers' fans. Once again quarterback Dan Fouts was master of the flight paths, throwing to an outstanding group of receivers who include Wes

End-of-season depth chart

OFFENSE

WR — 18 Charlie Joiner, 86 Jesse Bendross
OLT — 74 Jim Lachey, 65 Jerry Doerger
OLG — 67 Ed White, 63 Jim Leonard
C — 62 Don Macek, 66 Rich Umphrey
ORG — 63 Jim Leonard, 61 Ken Dallafior
ORT — 60 Dennis McKnight, 65 Jerry Doerger
TE — 80 Kellen Winslow, 85 Eric Sievers, 88 Pete Holohan
WR — 89 Wes Chandler, 83 Trumaine Johnson
QB — 14 Dan Fouts, 9 Mark Herrmann, 12 Joe Dufek
RB — 43 Tim Spencer, 21 Buford McGee, 31 Anthony Corley
RB — 26 Lionel James, 40 Gary Anderson

DEFENSE

DLE — 99 Lee Williams, 97 Tony Simmons
NT — 78 Chuck Ehin, 97 Tony Simmons, 92 Scott Garnett
DRE — 93 Earl Wilson, 90 Fred Robinson
LOLB — 57 Linden King, 53 Mike Guendling
LILB — 58 Mike Green, 55 Derrie Nelson, 56 Vince Osby
RILB — 56 Vince Osby, 55 Derrie Nelson
ROLB — 51 Woodrow Lowe, 53 Mike Guendling
LCB — 29 John Hendy, 20 Wayne Davis
RCB — 23 Danny Walters, 32 Terry Lewis
SS — 22 Gill Byrd, 27 Ronnie O'Bard
FS — 37 Jeff Dale, 24 Miles McPherson

SPECIAL TEAMS

P — 2 Ralf Mojsiejenko, 89 Wes Chandler
K — 16 Bob Thomas, 2 Ralf Mojsiejenko
H — 2 Ralf Mojsiejenko, 88 Pete Holohan
PR — 26 Lionel James, 40 Gary Anderson, 83 Trumaine Johnson
KR — 26 Lionel James, 40 Gary Anderson, 21 Buford McGee
LSN — 66 Rich Umphrey, 60 Dennis McKnight

ALSO WITH THE SAN DIEGO CHARGERS
42 Curtis Adams (RB), 6 Rolf Benirschke (K),
59 Craig Bingham (LB), 50 Carlos Bradley (LB),
77 Sam Claphan (T), 84 Chris Faulkner (TE),
79 Ron Faurot (DE), 52 Mark Fellows (LB),
75 Andrew Gissinger (T), 30 David King (CB),
68 Gary Kowalksi (T), 96 James Lockette (DE),
47 Bob Micho (TE), 59 Shane Nelson (LB),
39 Mark Schellen (RB), 64 Bill Searcey (G),
54 Billy Ray Smith (LB), 33 Lucious Smith (CB)

Chandler, Charlie Joiner, Lionel James and three top-notch tight ends. James, in fact, was a real bonus, finishing as the team's top rusher and breaking the club record for most combined yardage in a season.

But while this all-action offense blasted in scores from all directions, the defense was conceding them at a similar rate. No other team allowed as many total yards against as did San Diego. Coach Don Coryell has been wrestling with this problem for years, but he seems to be no nearer a solution. So it was no surprise that San Diego finished 8-8; that superb offense and dismal defense cancel each other out. You can't have one without the other. They won't be charging to the play-offs this time around, *unless* that defense sorts itself out.

Play-off prediction

2

Miami Dolphins' defenders, 1985:
above left quarterback Dan Marino (13), *above right* running back Tony Nathan (22)
below wide receivers Mark Clayton (83) and Mark Duper (85)

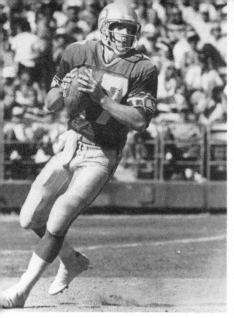

Dave Krieg (17)
Seattle Seahawks quarterback

Steve Largent (80)
wide receiver for the Seahawks

Bernie Kosar (19)
quarterback for the Cleveland Browns

Bill Walsh, head coach and president
of the San Francisco 49ers

Roger Craig, running back with the 49ers

1985 NEW YORK FOOTBALL GIANTS

First Row: ERIC SCHUBERT, SEAN LANDETA, ALI HAJI-SHEIKH (IR), PHIL SIMMS, JEFF RUTLEDGE, JOE MORRIS, TED WATTS, LEE ROUSON, PERRY WILLIAMS, KENNY DANIEL (IR), ROB CARPENTER, HERB WELCH, LARRY WINTERS (IR), TONY GALBREATH, GEORGE ADAMS, ELVIS PATTERSON, TERRY KINARD.

Second Row: SPECIAL TEAMS CAPTAIN ROBBIE JONES, DEFENSIVE CAPTAIN HARRY CARSON, ASST. COACHES: LEN FONTES, JOHNNY PARKER, MIKE SWEATMAN, LAMAR LEACHMAN, ROMEO CRENNEL, DEFENSIVE COORDINATOR BILL BELICHICK, HEAD COACH BILL PARCELLS, OFFENSIVE COORDINATOR RON ERHARDT, ASST. COACHES PAT HODGSON, MIKE POPE, RAY HANDLEY, FRED HOAGLIN, ANDY HEADEN, GARY REASONS, KENNY HILL, MAURICE CARTHON.

Third Row: LAWRENCE TAYLOR, BYRON HUNT, CARL BANKS, BRAD BENSON, CHRIS GODFREY, CONRAD GOODE, KARL NELSON, BART OATES, WILLIAM ROBERTS (IR), BILLY ARD, DAVID JORDAN, LEONARD MARSHALL, CASEY MERRILL, GORDON KING, GEORGE MARTIN.

Fourth Row: CURTIS McGRIFF, DAMIEN JOHNSON (IR), JEROME SALLY, DEE HARDISON, PHIL McCONKEY, JIM BURT, VYTO KAB (IR), ZEKE MOWATT (IR), DON HASSELBECK, LIONEL MANUEL, BYRON WILLIAMS, MARK BAVARO.

Fifth Row: HEAD TRAINER RONNIE BARNES, TRAINER JIM MADALENO, HEAD TRAINER EMERITUS JOHN DZIEGIEL, TRAINER JOHN JOHNSON, EQUIP. MGR. ED WAGNER, JR., LOCKER ROOM MGR. ED WAGNER, SR., FIELD SEC. MGR. JOE MANSFIELD, ASST. FILM COORDINATOR JOHN MANCUSO, FILM COORDINATOR TONY CEGLIO, STACY ROBINSON, TYRONE DAVIS (IR), MARK HAYNES (IR), BOBBY JOHNSON.

Eddie Johnson (51), linebacker for the Cleveland Browns

Tony Dorsett (33), a running back with the Dallas Cowboys

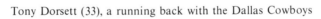

Houston Oilers quarterback
Warren Moon (1)

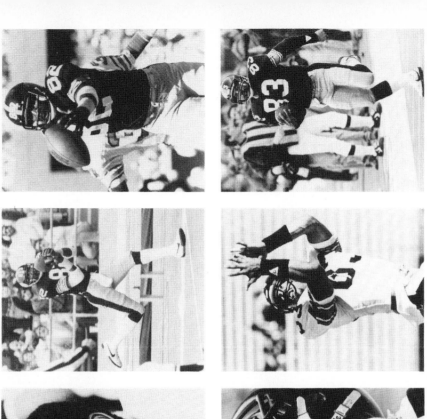

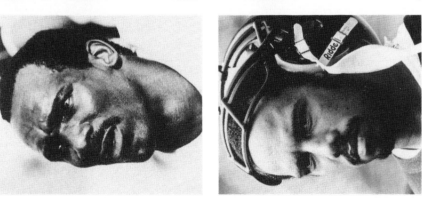

Two of the Pittsburgh Steelers'
wide receivers, John Stallworth (82)
and Louis Lipps (83)

Mick Luckhurst (18), the Atlanta Falcons' British kicker

Seattle Seahawks

AMERICAN FOOTBALL CONFERENCE — WESTERN DIVISION

Address:	5305 Lake Washington Boulevard, Kirkland, Washington 98033
Telephone:	(206) 827-9777
Colours:	Blue, green and silver
Stadium:	Kingdome, 201 South King Street, Seattle, Washington 98104
Capacity:	64,984
Playing surface:	AstroTurf

History

A mere $16 million bought the NFL franchise for Seattle Professional Football Inc., in 1974. But what about the nitty-gritty problem of a team name? Answer — a contest! 'Seahawks' was chosen from the 20,365 entries, having been suggested by some 151 people.

During their first season in 1976 the Seahawks won two games, and a year later in the Kingdome before 61,583 fans they established the record for the most wins ever by a second-year expansion team. In 1978, shedding the 'expansion team' tag, they finished 9-7, just one game off first place in the AFC West — not bad for year three! And 1979 saw a sensational rebound by the Seahawks, when after trailing 14-0, they pulled back to win 31-28 over Atlanta. Shown on ABC's 'Monday Night Football', it was undoubtedly a spectacular television debut.

Eight straight losses in the Kingdome in 1980 sent the

Seahawks into a tailspin. They plummeted all the way down, with their defense giving up 408 points — the most in the AFC.

In 1984 the Seahawks — for the first time in their franchise history — won the regular season opener. But at least it was something to squawk about — a resounding 33-0 victory over the poor Cleveland Browns. Later that year, Seattle eliminated Superbowl Champions, LA Raiders, from the play-offs in the AFC Wild Card game at Kingdome. However, they were themselves beaten less than a week later in the Divisional play-off game at the Orange Bowl by the Miami Dolphins, 31-17.

Last season

Just about everyone in the game felt positive about Seattle's chances last year. Some TV presenters even named them as Superbowl certs! But after a promising 1984, the Seahawks went flat in 1985. A superb 33-3 destruction of the Raiders raised early hopes, but a lack of consistency proved to be crucial.

Quarterback Dave Krieg has taken much of the stick, but this may be a little harsh on a young and daring player. Running back Kirk Warner returned after injury to rush up a 1,000-yard season, and receiver Steve Largent was again a joy to watch, yet somehow the offense just didn't seem to click.

But a much improved defense continued to impress and appears to have no serious fault. Coach Chuck Knox will be dismayed that this talented team flopped so badly last time out. Maybe they'll do what they have to in 1986.

Prediction

OK, so I was wrong last year. But I think the Seahawks have a lot going for them. They made mistakes last year, sure, but Knox and his team will learn from them. The Seahawks will be flying this time round.

Play-off prediction

8

Seattle Seahawks vs NFL

	Won	Lost	Tied
Atlanta	3	0	0
Buffalo	2	0	0
Chicago	3	1	0
Cincinnati	2	3	0
Cleveland	7	2	0
Dallas	0	3	0
Denver	7	11	0
Detroit	2	1	0
Green Bay	1	3	0
Houston	2	3	0
Indianapolis	0	2	0
Kansas City	7	8	0
Los Angeles Raiders	9	9	0
Los Angeles Rams	0	3	0
Miami	1	3	0
Minnesota	2	1	0
New England	1	5	0
New Orleans	2	1	0
New York Giants	1	3	0
New York Jets	7	1	0
Philadelphia	0	2	0
Pittsburgh	2	3	0
San Diego	6	9	0
San Francisco	2	1	0
St Louis	0	2	0
Tampa Bay	2	0	0
Washington	1	2	0

End-of-season depth chart

OFFENSE

WR	— 81 Daryl Turner, 82 Paul Skansi, 83 Ray Butler
OLT	— 71 Bryan Millard, 76 Jon Borchardt
OLG	— 65 Edwin Bailey, 71 Bryan Millard
C	— 59 Blair Bush, 62 Kani Kauahi
ORG	— 61 Robert Pratt, 71 Bryan Millard
ORT	— 78 Bob Cryder, 76 Jon Borchardt
TE	— 87 Charle Young, 85 Dan Ross, 86 Mike Tice
WR	— 80 Steve Largent, 89 Byron Walker
QB	— 17 Dave Krieg, 7 Gale Gilbert
RB	— 28 Curt Warner, 43 Randall Morris, 37 Eric Lane
RB	— 46 David Hughes, 37 Eric Lane, 29 Rick Parros

DEFENSE

DLE	— 79 Jacob Green, 68 Randy Edwards
NT	— 72 Joe Nash, 63 Reggie Kinlaw
DRE	— 77 Jeff Bryant, 68 Randy Edwards
LOLB	— 58 Bruce Scholtz, 54 John Kaiser
LILB	— 50 Fredd Young, 57 Shelton Robinson
RILB	— 53 Keith Butler, 51 Sam Merriman
ROLB	— 55 Michael Jackson, 56 Greg Gaines
LCB	— 20 Terry Taylor, 42 Keith Simpson
RCB	— 22 Dave Brown, 24 Terry Jackson
SS	— 45 Kenny Easley, 21 Paul Moyer, 41 Eugene Robinson
FS	— 44 John Harris, 21 Paul Moyer, 41 Eugene Robinson

SPECIAL TEAMS

P	— 15 Dave Finzer
K	— 9 Norm Johnson
H	— 7 Gale Gilbert, 80 Steve Largent
PR	— 82 Paul Skansi, 45 Kenny Easeley
KR	— 43 Randall Morris, 82 Paul Skansi
LSN	— 59 Blair Bush, 62 Kani Kauahi

ALSO WITH THE SEATTLE SEAHAWKS
Tony Davis (TE), 33 Dan Doornink (RB), 64 Ron Essink (T),
88 Byron Franklin (WR), 84 Danny Greene (WR)

National Football Conference

Atlanta Falcons

NATIONAL FOOTBALL CONFERENCE — WESTERN DIVISION

Address:	1-85 Suwanee Road, Suwanee, Georgia, 30174
Telephone:	(404) 588-1111
Colours:	Red, black, white and silver
Stadium:	Atlanta-Fulton County Stadium, 521 Capitol Avenue S.W., Atlanta, Georgia 30312
Capacity:	60,748
Playing surface:	Grass

History

'Doesn't every adult made in America want to own his own football team?', was Rankin M. Smith's answer to why, in 1965, he bought the Atlanta Falcons, paying approximately $8,500,000 for the NFL franchise. And if you own a football team, you naturally want to name it too. Smith called the Atlanta Falcons after his five children and registered the team under the corporate name of 'Five Smiths Incorporated.'

A special day for the Falcons came on 30 November 1966 — their first victory! Taking on the New York Giants, they came through with a score of 27-16. Less than two weeks later, with the taste of success still fresh, they beat St Louis 16-10 in Atlantic Stadium, their first victory before the delighted home crowd.

103

When the Falcons opened the 1969 season by convincingly crushing San Francisco 21-7, it pointed the way to a winning streak. They went on to defeat Minnesota 10-7, and put an end to the Vikings' twelve-game run. They closed the season with a 6-8-1 record — the best in the club's history. But they had to wait until 1971 for their first winning season, 7-6-1, for which credit must go to the wide receiver Ken Burrow, in particular for a touchdown pass from quarterback Bob Berry in a 24-20 victory over New Orleans.

In 1973 Berry was traded before the start of an eventful season. Quarterback Dick Skinner gave Atlanta the extra zest they needed, overwhelming New Orleans 62-7 in the opening game, the Falcons set a total of 35 team records. They stunned the unbeaten Minnesota Vikings 20-14 and a 28-20 victory over the New York Jets was Atlanta's seventh consecutive triumph. Sadly, they then missed the play-offs by losing two of their last three games!

Kitted out with new feathers (the uniforms still worn by the team), in 1978 the Falcons recorded the first-ever shut-out in Atlanta-Fulton County Stadium, beating Detroit 14-0, and received their first-ever play-off berth when Washington was beaten by Chicago.

On 24 December, quarterback Steve Bartowski threw two touchdown passes in the last eight minutes to squeeze Atlanta past Philadelphia in the NFC Wild Card, 13-14. But six days later they lost 27-20 to Dallas.

In 1980 the Falcons were flying again, clinching their first NFC Western Division title, but in their second play-off appearance they stumbled against Dallas in a close-fought 30-27 game. The year 1982 saw Atlanta in the play-offs again, but they fell at the first fence, losing to the Vikings 30-24.

And let's hear it for an Englishman, Mick Luckhurst, Atlanta's kicker — who on 9 September 1984 became the Falcons' all-time leading scorer. In 1984 the Falcons sustained two major injuries: on 7 October Billy 'Whiteshoes' Johnson sustained a knee injury, and on 18 November Steve Bartowski suffered the same fate, and both men were out of action for the year.

Atlanta Falcons vs NFL

	Won	Lost	Tied
Buffalo	2	2	0
Chicago	9	5	0
Cincinnati	1	4	0
Cleveland	1	6	0
Dallas	1	8	0
Denver	3	3	0
Detroit	4	12	0
Green Bay	6	8	0
Houston	4	1	0
Indianapolis	0	8	0
Kansas City	0	2	0
Los Angeles Raiders	1	4	0
Los Angeles Rams	8	28	2
Miami	0	4	0
Minnesota	6	9	0
New England	2	2	0
New Orleans	23	11	0
New York Giants	6	5	0
New York Jets	2	1	0
Philadelphia	6	6	1
Pittsburgh	1	6	0
San Diego	2	0	0
San Francisco	17	21	0
St Louis	3	6	0
Seattle	0	3	0
Tampa Bay	2	3	0
Washington	2	9	1

Last season

At one stage it looked as if the Falcons would finish with the worst record in the entire NFL. That they avoided this

End-of-season depth chart

OFFENSE

WR	—	82 Stacey Bailey, 81 Billy Johnson, 85 Anthony Allen
OLT	—	67 Eric Sanders, 55 Wayne Radloff
OLG	—	63 Jeff Kiewel, 66 Chuck Thomas
C	—	57 Jeff Van Note, 55 Wayne Radloff, 66 Chuck Thomas
ORG	—	79 Bill Fralic, 66 Chuck Thomas
ORT	—	62 Brett Miller, 71 Glen Howe, 79 Bill Fralic
TE	—	88 Arthur Cox, 49 Al Matthews
WR	—	89 Charlie Brown, 81 Billy Johnson, 85 Anthony Allen
QB	—	16 Dave Archer, 8 Bob Holly
HB	—	87 Cliff Benson, 45 Ken Whisenhunt, 81 Billy Johnson
RB	—	42 Gerald Riggs, 24 Joe Washington, 29 Sylvester Stamps, 32 Tim Tyrrell

DEFENSE

DLE	—	77 Rick Bryan, 72 Andrew Provence
DLT	—	74 Mike Pitts, 70 Willard Goff
DRT	—	69 Dan Benish, 70 Willard Goff
DRE	—	76 Mike Gann, 72 Andrew Provence
LLB	—	59 John Rade, 96 Johnny Taylor, 53 Thomas Benson
MLB	—	50 Buddy Curry, 92 Ronnie Washington, 53 Thomas Benson
RLB	—	56 Al Richardson, 58 David Frye, 53 Thomas Benson
LCB	—	23 Bobby Butler, 30 David Croudip
RCB	—	20 Wendell Cason, 30 David Croudip
LS	—	25 Scott Case, 37 Kenny Johnson, 22 Sean Thomas
RS	—	27 Tom Pridemore, 36 Danny Wagoner

SPECIAL TEAMS

P	—	1 Ralph Giacomarro, 18 Mick Luckhurst
K	—	18 Mick Luckhurst
H	—	16 Dave Archer, 24 Joe Washington
PR	—	85 Anthony Allen, 81 Billy Johnson, 24 Joe Washington
KR	—	36 Danny Wagoner, 29 Sylvester Stamps, 85 Anthony Allen
LSN	—	67 Eric Sanders, 57 Jeff Van Note

ALSO WITH THE ATLANTA FALCONS
31 William Andrews (RB), 39 Cliff Austin (RB), 38 John Ayres (DB),
26 James Britt (CB), 3 Rick Donnelly (P), 33 Tiger Greene (CB),
78 Mike Kenn (T), 80 Mike Landrum (DB), 52 Rydell Malancon (LB),
93 Brent Martin (C), 64 Joe Pellegrini (C/G), 61 John Scully (G)

ignominy is largely a tribute to the ground-gaining ability of Gerald Riggs.

Atlanta are another team with quarterback problems. Dave Archer holds the starter's job now, but he lacked experience and a leaky offensive line meant that he had little time to learn his trade. Receiver Billy 'Whiteshoes' Johnson had another good year (breaking the NFL record for punch return yardage), although the good form of tight end Arthur Cox was a real surprise.

There are a number of defensive problems. The line does not rush the passer adequately and the secondary was badly exposed on several occasions. One bright spot for Falcon fans was the consistent form of British kicker Mick Luckhurst. But when your only decent player is a kicker, then you finish 4-12.

Prediction

Don't expect the Falcons to be flying high this year. Quarterback Dave Archer needs time to gain his confidence, but with a bit of help from the draft they should improve on their 4-12 record of last season.

Play-off prediction

2

Chicago Bears

NATIONAL FOOTBALL CONFERENCE — CENTRAL DIVISION

Address:	Halas Hall, 250 North Washington, Lake Forest, Illinois 60045
Telephone:	(312) 295-6600
Colours:	Navy blue, orange and white
Stadium:	Soldier Field, 425 McFetridge Place, Chicago, Illinois 60605
Capacity:	65,790
Playing surface:	AstroTurf

History

Back in 1920 the small town of Decatur, Illinois didn't have a lot going for it. One of the town's few claims to fame was a starch factory owned by a Mr A.E.Staley. He hired a 25-year-old not only to work making starch, but also to play in his semi-pro baseball team and organize a company football squad. This young man was to become the most important influence on the development of modern American Football. From a starch factory, to the Hall of Fame... George Halas.

Halas was promised a big enough budget to attract top players *and* he was allowed to practise in company time. To begin with all went well, but in 1921 the starch business went slack and with profits dwindling Staley withdrew his money from his football team but suggested that Halas take it over. Halas agreed and moved the team to Chicago and for a fee of $5,000 he agreed to call the team the 'Chicago Staleys' for one

109

year. That year was a good one for Halas and the Staleys — they won the American Professional Football Association championship 10-1-1 and, although runners-up Buffalo protested that the Staleys' score included non-league games (they were overruled), the team from the starch factory were on their way.

His contract with Staley now at an end, Halas renamed the team. He had just done a deal for his team to play at Cub Park, so he chose a name appropriate to their new home. The Bears were born on 28 January 1922, and at Halas's suggestion the APFA got a new name as well . . . the National Football League.

In their first season the Bears did well, finishing second with a 9-3 record *and* the team made a healthy profit of $1,476. In 1925 Halas made a significant signing that would eventually take the Bears to greatness. He signed a young man from the University of Illinois, his name Red Grange. His agent C.C. ('Cash and Carry') Pyle got Halas to part with $100,000 for Red's services, a fortune at the time.

In 1930, in an exhibition game to help the unemployed, the Bears played the first *indoor* American Football game against the Cardinals on an eighty-yard field at Chicago Stadium — and it was there two years later, helped by a touchdown from Red Grange, that the Bears won the NFC Championship.

If you want to put a date on the beginning of pro football's modern era, 8 December 1940 is as good as any. It was then that in an astonishing annihilation of Washington, 73-0, Halas unveiled the revolutionary 'T' formation that would prompt other clubs quickly to adopt the same attack. Three weeks earlier, in a regular season game without the T-formation, the Bears had lost to the Redskins 7-3.

In 1950 the All American Football Conference collapsed and the NFL restructured itself into two Conferences, the National and the American, and the Bears became one of seven teams in the National Football Conference, finishing second with a 9-4 record.

In 1955 Halas announced that he would retire from coaching in favour of a younger man, and for the 1956 season Paddy Driscoll, Halas's assistant, became head coach (Driscoll was only two years younger than Halas). The Bears did well but lost the NFL Championship game to the Giants; because of the icy

110

Chicago Bears vs NFL

	Won	Lost	Tied
Atlanta	5	9	0
Buffalo	2	1	0
Cincinnati	0	2	0
Cleveland	2	6	0
Dallas	4	8	0
Denver	4	3	0
Detroit	64	44	5
Green Bay	70	55	6
Houston	1	2	0
Indianapolis	14	21	0
Kansas City	2	1	0
Los Angeles Raiders	1	4	0
Los Angeles Rams	43	27	3
Miami	0	4	0
Minnesota	22	25	2
New England	3	2	0
New Orleans	4	4	1
New York Giants	27	16	2
New York Jets	2	1	0
Philadelphia	19	4	1
Pittsburgh	13	4	1
San Diego	1	4	0
San Francisco	24	23	1
St Louis	50	25	6
Seattle	1	3	0
Tampa Bay	12	4	0
Washington	20	11	1

conditions in Yankee Stadium the Giants wore tennis shoes for greater traction, the sneakers worked wonders and the Bears were tamed 47-7. Halas, however, could not keep away from coaching and returned in 1958 — he stayed for another ten years

End-of-season depth chart

OFFENSE

WR	—	83 Willie Gault, 82 Ken Margerum, 89 Keith Ortego
OLT	—	74 Jim Covert, 71 Andy Frederick
OLG	—	62 Mark Bortz, 75 Stefan Humphries
C	—	63 Jay Hilgenberg, 60 Tom Andrews, 57 Tom Thayer
ORG	—	57 Tom Thayer, 75 Stefan Humphries
ORT	—	78 Keith Van Horne, 71 Andy Frederick
TE	—	87 Emery Moorehead, 80 Tim Wrightman
WR	—	85 Dennis McKinnon, 82 Ken Margerum
QB	—	9 Jim McMahon, 4 Steve Fuller, 18 Mike Tomczak
RB	—	26 Matt Suhey, 33 Calvin Thomas
RB	—	34 Walter Payton, 29 Dennis Gentry, 20 Thomas Sanders

DEFENSE

DLE	—	99 Dan Hampton, 73 Mike Hartenstine
DLT	—	76 Steve McMichael, 72 William Perry, 70 Henry Waechter
DRT	—	72 William Perry, 99 Dan Hampton, 70 Henry Waechter
DRE	—	95 Richard Dent, 98 Tyrone Keys, 70 Henry Waechter
LLB	—	55 Otis Wilson, 52 Cliff Thrift, 59 Ron Rivera
MLB	—	50 Mike Singletary, 52 Cliff Thrift, 54 Brian Cabral
RLB	—	58 Wilber Marshall, 59 Ron Rivera, 51 Jim Morrissey
LCB	—	27 Mike Richardson, 48 Reggie Phillips, 23 Shaun Gayle
RCB	—	21 Leslie Frazier, 31 Ken Taylor, 23 Shaun Gayle
SS	—	22 Dave Duerson, 23 Shaun Gayle
FS	—	45 Gary Fencik, 23 Shaun Gayle

SPECIAL TEAMS

P	—	8 Maury Buford
K	—	6 Kevin Butler
H	—	4 Steve Fuller, 18 Mike Tomczak
PR	—	89 Keith Ortego, 31 Ken Taylor, 85 Dennis McKinnon
KR	—	83 Willie Gault, 29 Dennis Gentry, 31 Ken Taylor
LSN	—	63 Jay Hilgenberg, 57 Tom Thayer

ALSO WITH THE CHICAGO BEARS
86 Brad Anderson (WR), 84 Brian Baschnagel (WR),
79 Kurt Becker (G), 88 Pat Dunsmore (TE), 24 Jeff Fisher (DB),
Mitch Krenk (TE), 81 James Maness (WR), 53 Dan Rains (LB),
67 Joe Rammuno (G/C)

and retired after forty seasons as the winningest coach in Football history, with 326 wins, 150 defeats and 30 ties.

In 1971 the Bears took up residence at Soldier Field on the banks of Lake Michigan and in doing so won five of their first seven games.

Walter Payton, a running back, was drafted in 1975 but Chicago finished with a 4-10 record, their seventh consecutive losing season. The following year Payton began to show the beginnings of his greatness leading the NFL with 1,390 yards and, despite losing to Dallas the following season in the first round of the play-offs, Payton set a new Bears record with 1,852 yards rushing.

On 31 October 1983 'Papa Bear' George Halas died at the age of 88. The Bears today believe that he still guides them, for in 1984 they clinched their first Divisional title since 1963; and as we know Papa Bear was with them all the way through last year's near-perfect season.

Last season

What more can one say about the team that's got it all? The Superbowl Champion Bears are so strong that they can even afford the luxury of using gifted running back Walter Payton as a decoy for William 'The Refrigerator' Perry!

It is pointless attempting to highlight any particular areas or players. Their rushing defense, orchestrated by Richard Dent, is probably the most effective unit ever witnessed in the NFL. What makes Chicago tick is that they play as a team and you can find truly gifted individuals in almost every position. We all know about Perry, Payton, Dent, Jim McMahon and company. The point is, these superstars are supported by quality throughout the roster.

There is one question mark. Will the departure of Defensive Coordinator Buddy Ryan affect them? Well, it's difficult to see how they are going to get any better.

Prediction

I have already put money on them to be at the Rosebowl, Pasadena in Superbowl XXI.

113

Play-off prediction

10

Dallas Cowboys

NATIONAL FOOTBALL CONFERENCE — EASTERN DIVISION

Address:	One Cowboy Parkway, Irving, Texas, 75063
Telephone:	(214) 369-8000
Colours:	Royal blue, metallic silver, blue and white
Stadium:	Texas Stadium, Irving, Texas 75062
Capacity:	63,749
Playing surface:	*Texas* Turf
Special Note:	The Cowboys have a 'Dial a Cowboy' service on (214) 487-1111. Dial that number during the season to hear a tape interview with a player or coach . . . British Telecom will love you!

History

In 26 years they've been in the play-offs 18 times, winning five NFC titles for a record five Superbowl appearances — their guide, architect, and mentor is second only to George Halas as the all-time winningest coach in NFL history — Tom Landry, a former bomber pilot in World War Two, has made the Cowboys 'America's Team'.

The Cowboys came into being on 28 January 1960, and Landry was appointed head coach; one of his first signings was a young quarterback called Don Meredith. Playing their home games at the Cottonbowl in that first season they lost their first 10 league games before tying to New York Giants 31-31. Landry was always an innovator, and in 1962 he unveiled the 'shuttling

115

quarterback offense'. Landry let his two quarterbacks, Eddie Le Baron and Don Meredith, play alternate downs. It worked a treat, with the Cowboys winning four of their first eight games, but an injury to Le Baron against the New York Giants crippled the Dallas offense, and they won only one of their last six games.

In 1966 it all started to come together, Landry building his team with great skill, and on 1 January 1967 the Cowboys met the mighty Green Bay Packers in what was one of the most thrilling championship games in NFL history. Dallas lost 34-27, but the following season they had another crack at the Packers on one of the coldest days in Green Bay history, the temperature −13°! The Cowboys fought the Packers for the NFL Championship — in the final seconds, Green Bay won 21-17. Landry's comment: 'You can tell the real Cowboys, the ones with the frost-bitten fingers, and the broken hearts.'

In 1970 the Cowboys showed their class, battling from a 5-4 record they won their last five games, and in beating San Francisco 17-10 in the NFC Championship game they went to the Orangebowl, Miami to meet the Baltimore Colts in Superbowl V. It was a game marked by eleven fumbles and interceptions and fourteen penalties. With six minutes and 35 seconds left in the game, the score was 13-13; but after an interception by Baltimore the ball was on the Cowboys' 25 with nine seconds to go. Jim O'Brien, Baltimore's kicker, won it for the Colts with a 32-yard field goal — the Cowboys were stunned and dismayed — they just could not win 'the big one'. But they did the next year. After a disappointing start, Dallas met Miami in Superbowl VI in New Orleans and with their quarterback Roger Staubach completing 12 of 19 passes and Duane Thomas rushing for 95 yards, the Cowboys buried the Dolphins 24-3. The Dolphins even had a little advice from the President of the United States himself, Richard M. Nixon. He telephoned Don Schula and said, 'The Cowboys are a good defensive team, but I think you can hit Paul Warfield (the Dolphins' star wide receiver) on that down and out pattern.' Someone must have been listening to President Nixon's conversation! The Cowboys double-teamed Warfield and he just couldn't run his pattern. The Cowboys had finally cracked it. Superbowl Rings were theirs and each man was richer by $15,000.

Dallas Cowboys vs NFL

	Won	Lost	Tied
Atlanta	8	1	0
Buffalo	3	1	0
Chicago	8	4	0
Cincinnati	2	1	0
Cleveland	9	15	0
Denver	3	1	0
Detroit	6	3	0
Green Bay	5	8	0
Houston	4	1	0
Indianapolis	6	3	0
Kansas City	2	1	0
Los Angeles Raiders	1	2	0
Los Angeles Rams	10	10	0
Miami	2	3	0
Minnesota	10	5	0
New England	5	0	0
New Orleans	11	1	0
New York Giants	32	13	2
New York Jets	3	0	0
Philadelphia	34	17	0
Pittsburgh	11	12	0
San Diego	2	1	0
San Francisco	8	8	1
St Louis	29	17	1
Seattle	3	0	0
Tampa Bay	6	0	0
Washington	30	20	2

In 1975 Landry revitalized the shotgun offense with Roger Staubach taking the snap eight yards behind the centre. This new-look offense worked a treat and they secured the NFC Wild Card spot. It was a close game against Minnesota, but

End-of-season depth chart

OFFENSE

WR	—	80 Tony Hill, 81 Karl Powe, 87 Gordon Banks
OLT	—	66 Chris Schultz, 70 Howard Richards, 71 Mark Tuinei
OLG	—	63 Glen Titensor, 67 Broderick Thompson, 70 Howard Richards
C	—	64 Tom Rafferty, 71 Mark Tuinei, 63 Glen Titensor
ORG	—	65 Kurt Petersen, 67 Broderick Thompson, 70 Howard Richards
ORT	—	61 Jim Cooper, 75 Phil Pozderac, 71 Mark Tuinei
TE	—	84 Doug Cosbie, 85 Fred Cornwell, 89 Brian Salonen
WR	—	82 Mike Renfro, 81 Karl Powe, 86 Kenny Duckett
QB	—	11 Danny White, 14 Gary Hogeboom, 16 Steve Pelluer
RB	—	33 Tony Dorsett, 23 James Jones, 30 Timmy Newsome
RB	—	30 Timmy Newsome, 46 Todd Fowler, 23 James Jones

DEFENSE

DLE	—	72 Ed Jones, 99 Kevin Brooks, 60 Don Smerek
DLT	—	78 John Dutton, 60 Don Smerek, 99 Kevin Brooks
DRT	—	54 Randy White, 60 Don Smerek, 99 Kevin Brooks
DRE	—	77 Jim Jeffcoat, 99 Kevin Brooks, 60 Don Smerek
LLB	—	58 Mike Hegman, 89 Brian Salonen, 36 Vince Albritton
MLB	—	56 Eugene Lockhart, 55 Steve De Ossie, 50 Jeff Rohrer
RLB	—	50 Jeff Rohrer, 59 Jesse Penn, 36 Vince Albritton
LCB	—	24 Everson Walls, 22 Victor Scott, 32 Dennis Thurman
RCB	—	27 Ron Fellows, 22 Victor Scott, 32 Dennis Thurman
SS	—	47 Dextor Clinkscale, 40 Bill Bates, 32 Dennis Thurman
FS	—	26 Michael Downs, 32 Dennis Thurman, 40 Bill Bates

SPECIAL TEAMS

P	—	4 Mike Saxon, 11 Danny White
K	—	1 Rafael Septien, 4 Mike Saxon
H	—	14 Gary Hogeboom, 16 Steve Pelluer
PR	—	87 Gordon Banks, 40 Bill Bates, 23 James Jones
KR	—	86 Kenny Duckett, 23 James Jones, 81 Karl Powe
LSN(P)	—	55 Steve De Ossie, 64 Tom Rafferty
LSN(F)	—	64 Tom Rafferty, 55 Steve De Ossie

ALSO WITH THE DALLAS COWBOYS
76 Dowe Aughtman (G), 62 Brian Baldinger (G), 83 Leon Gonzalez (WR), 68 Crawford Ker (G), 29 Robert Lavette (RB), 98 Kurt Ploeger (DE), 43 Ronald Story (RB), 94 Chris Waltman (TE)

118

Dallas won it 17-14 with twenty-four seconds left as Staubach threw a fifty-yarder to Drew Pearson.

In the NFC Championship the Cowboys whipped the Rams 37-7 and their defense had a magnificent day, not allowing the Rams to cross midfield until the end of the third quarter. Dallas were in the Superbowl again. In Superbowl X, despite leading most of the way, they lost to the Steelers 21-17.

On 15 January 1978 they were in Louisiana Superdome, contesting Superbowl XII against the Denver Broncos, and for the first half the Cowboys' defense dominated, intercepting four passes and recovering three fumbles. They led 13-0 at the half and went on to win 27-10.

The following year the Cowboys nearly did it again, but the Steelers held on to win Superbowl XIII 35-31. It was after that season that the Cowboys became 'America's Team'. They used that as the title for their highlight film, and this little piece of modesty stuck.

In 1980 Roger Staubach announced his retirement after 11 record-breaking years with the Cowboys, and behind their new quarterback Danny White the Cowboys notched up their 15th consecutive winning season with a 12-4 record. They were in the play-offs for the 14th time in 15 years, but lost to the Eagles 20-7 in the Championship game.

In 1981 they were in the play-offs again for the second year in a row, but Dallas lost the Conference Championship game when San Francisco narrowly beat them 28-27. In 1984 the Cowboys defeated the Eagles 26-10 to extend their NFL record but missed the play-offs for the first time in 10 years.

Last season

Once again the Cowboys had one of those seasons when success seemed to be just beyond them. When they were good — as against Washington — they were superb. But when they were bad (remember Cincinnati and Chicago?) they were awful. Inconsistency has been the Cowboys' bugbear throughout the decade.

But at least in 1985 quarterback Danny White repaid coach Landry's faith in his ability and registered an improved campaign. His favourite receiver, Tony Hill, and tight end Doug

Cosbie, kept it moving in the air, and running back Tony Dorsett put his off-pitch problems behind him to keep the ground attack lively. A much improved line gave White the time and space he needs to do his stuff. And despite the occasional hiccup the defense stayed tough. Special teams emerged as a big problem area, and one that will have to be addressed if Dallas want to repeat their play-off appearance in 1986.

Prediction

Tom Landry wants to go to the Superbowl before he retires. He is being wooed by the Republican Party for political office. But I think America's Team will be back in the play-offs, though whether they reach the Superbowl...

Play-off Prediction

8

Detroit Lions

NATIONAL FOOTBALL CONFERENCE — CENTRAL DIVISION

Address:	Pontiac Silverdome, 1200 Featherstone Road, Pontiac, Michigan 48057
Telephone:	(313) 335-4131
Colours:	Honolulu blue and silver
Stadium:	Pontiac Silverdome (*address as above*)
Capacity:	80,638
Playing surface:	AstroTurf

History

Reformed in 1933, the new Detroit Lions found immediate success, winning 10 straight games including seven consecutive shut-outs. Defeat came first against Green Bay, 3-0; then, playing their first traditional Thanksgiving Day home game, the Lions lost to the Bears, 19-16; not much there for the 26,000-strong home supporters to give thanks for. The Lions did, however, redeem themselves the following year, knocking the New York Giants down to size and taking the Championship with a 26-7 score. Moving to a new lair in Briggs Stadium wasn't a roaring success, but the Lions managed a gentle, satisfying purr, beating Pittsburgh 16-7 in their first match on home territory. There was cat-fighting behind the scenes, with Hall of Famer Dutch Clark accusing owner George Richards of 'meddling'. Nevertheless the Lions in those early years established themselves as an integral part of the Michigan football scene.

121

In 1939 the Lions were sold to a department store magnate, Fred Mandel, for a reported sum of $225,000. Eight years later the team was sold again, by a now disappointed and dispirited Mandel, for a significantly low figure of $185,000. The Lions next became the pet of a group of local businessmen; during the syndicate's control which lasted until 1964, the Lions on a number of occasions showed their claws. They beat Los Angeles Rams 31-21 in 1952 to take the NFL National Conference title, and that same year won their first Championship since 1935, beating the Cleveland Browns on their home ground 17-7. A third Championship quickly followed in 1953, and in 1957 a fourth.

The Lions were transferred from the syndicate to a sole owner — William Clay Ford, for a price of $4.5 million — and once again the big-cat fighting was rife, culminating in 1966 with the Vikings and the Lions tied for last position in the Western Conference. The year 1967 was little better, with the Lions becoming the first NFL team to be beaten by an AFL team (Denver vs Lions 13-7).

The 1976 move to the Silverdome, the world's largest air-supported dome structure, produced just one win in four games for the Lions, and it wasn't until 1982 that they finally made the play-offs — for the first time since 1970. The NFC Central Division crown was theirs in 1983, but they were beaten by San Francisco 24-23 in the first round of the play-offs. In 1984 their record was an abysmal four wins, 11 losses and one tie.

Last season

The Lions were almost unbeatable at home, losing only to Chicago. But on the road, they were toothless, losing to every team they faced. Coach Daryl Roagers, who did well in his first NFL campaign, needs to correct this frightening imbalance.

Eric Hipple was handed the starting quarterback job and he grabbed it with both hands. So too did receiver Leonard Thompson, who was partnered effectively by Mark Nichols. Running back Billy Simms failed to return from injury, but James Jones was able to take up much of the slack.

It was a tale of two teams on defense. The Detroit side could handle most pass attacks comfortably (take a bow, Bobby

122

Detroit Lions vs NFL

	Won	Lost	Tied
Atlanta	12	4	0
Buffalo	1	1	1
Chicago	44	64	5
Cincinnati	2	1	0
Cleveland	12	3	0
Dallas	3	6	0
Denver	2	3	0
Green Bay	47	57	6
Houston	1	2	0
Indianapolis	16	17	2
Kansas City	2	2	0
Los Angeles Raiders	2	3	0
Los Angeles Rams	34	36	1
Miami	1	2	0
Minnesota	17	30	2
New England	2	2	0
New Orleans	4	4	1
New York Giants	18	11	1
New York Jets	2	2	0
Philadelphia	2	9	2
Pittsburgh	13	8	1
San Diego	3	2	0
San Francisco	26	23	1
St Louis	25	15	5
Seattle	1	2	0
Tampa Bay	9	7	0
Washington	8	19	0

Watkins), but the front seven, which was changed to 3-4 at the start of the campaign by Roagers, looked ill at ease when facing a fast-paced rushing attack.

End-of-season depth chart

OFFENSE

WR	—	39 Leonard Thompson, 82 Pete Mandley
OLT	—	75 Lomas Brown, 71 Rich Strenger
OLG	—	72 Chris Dieterich, 67 Don Greco, 65 Mark Stevenson
C	—	52 Steve Mott, 65 Mark Stevenson, 60 Tom Turnure
ORG	—	70 Keith Dorney, 67 Don Greco, 65 Mark Stevenson
ORT	—	71 Rich Strenger, 70 Keith Dorney
TE	—	87 David Lewis, 84 Rob Rubick, 81 Reese McCall
WR	—	80 Carl Bland, 82 Pete Mandley
QB	—	17 Eric Hipple, 12 Joe Ferguson
RB	—	24 Alvin Moore, 34 A.J. Jones
RB	—	30 James Jones, 32 Rick Kane, 36 Mike Meade

DEFENSE

DLE	—	77 Keith Ferguson, 66 Leon Evans, 63 Martin Moss
NT	—	62 Curtis Green, 68 Steve Baack, 63 Martin Moss
DRE	—	79 William Gay, 77 Keith Ferguson, 63 Martin Moss
LOLB	—	59 Jimmy Williams, 96 June James
LILB	—	57 Ken Fantetti, 97 Dan Bunz
RILB	—	50 August Curley, 97 Dan Bunz
ROLB	—	92 Angelo King, 98 Vernon Maxwell, 54 Roosevelt Barnes
LCB	—	27 Bobby Watkins, 42 John Bostic
RCB	—	29 Bruce McNorton, 42 John Bostic, 40 Duane Galloway
SS	—	21 Demetrious Johnson, 35 Alvin Hall, 26 William Frizzell
FS	—	33 William Graham, 35 Alvin Hall, 26 William Frizzell

SPECIAL TEAMS

P	—	11 Mike Black, 3 Eddie Murray
K	—	3 Eddie Murray, 11 Mike Black
H	—	17 Eric Hipple, 11 Mike Black
PR	—	82 Pete Mandley, 35 Alvin Hall
KR	—	82 Pete Mandley, 35 Alvin Hall, 34 A.J. Jones
LSN	—	60 Tom Turnure, 63 Martin Moss

ALSO WITH THE DETROIT LIONS

95 Kurt Allerman (LB), Clayton Beauford (WR), 23 Arnold Brown (CB), 89 Jeff Chadwick (WR), 55 Mike Cofer (LB), 44 Dave D'Addio (RB), 93 Kirk Dodge (LB), 78 Doug English (NT), 53 Kevin Glover (C/G), Kevin Hancock (LB), 58 James Harrell (LB), James Johnson (LB), 51 David Jones (C/G), 73 Don Laster (T), 14 Mike Machurek (QB), 28 Wilbert Montgomery (RB), 86 Mark Nichols (WR), 20 Billy Sims (RB), Ray Snell (G), 76 Eric Williams (NT)

Prediction

Seven wins and nine losses, that was Detroit's record in the NFC Central last year. They should improve on that. But I think the only way they will be seeing post-season play is on their television sets.

Play-off prediction

3

Green Bay Packers

NATIONAL FOOTBALL CONFERENCE — CENTRAL DIVISION

Address:	1265 Lombardi Avenue, Green Bay, Wisconsin 54307-0628
Telephone:	(414) 494-2351
Colours:	Dark green, gold and white
Stadia:	Lambeau Field, PO Box 10628, 1265 Lombardi Avenue, Green Bay, Wisconsin 54307-0628
	Milwaukee County Stadium Highway 1-94, Milwaukee, Wisconsin 53214
Capacity:	56,926 (Lambeau Field); 55, 976 (Milwaukee County)
Playing surface:	Grass

History

'Why not get up a football team?' That casual comment between friends Earl (Curly) Lambeau and George Calhoun was the beginning of the incredible legend of the Green Bay Packers. Nothing could be more modest than the early days of the Packers — the small-town team which gained worldwide recognition by winning, over the next fifty years, more Championships than any other team in pro football. Lambeau was just home from school when he and Calhoun met and chatted about football on a street corner in 1919. It was a fateful discussion. Lambeau had just started working for the India Packing Company and, fired with enthusiasm, quickly talked his employers into putting up money for some equipment. Providing the team jerseys and letting the players use their athletics field for practice, the company and footballers were linked in early publicity, and the team were dubbed 'the Packers'. The name stuck and on 11 August 1919 the Green Bay Packers were launched from the dingy offices of the *Green Bay Press Gazette*. The early days were successful, but frugal. Not only were there no ushers, no majorettes, and no band, at first there were also no fences, no gates, and *no entrance charge*! Fans simply passed round the hat and on its scant contents the team subsisted. But, winning 10 out of 11 games in their first season, the Packers in 1921 obtained a franchise in the newly-formed National Pro-Football League. A big step, but the gates didn't pay the freight, and at the end of the season the franchise was sadly forfeited. Troubles then began to mount, despite Lambeau finding a new backer and buying back the franchise. Even the weather was against them, and it really didn't seem quite fair that the financially struggling team should lose out to a large insurance company. Torrential rain had caused a fixture to be cancelled but the official amount of water measured was a tiny one-hundredth of an inch short of the policy requirement — the insurers refused to pay up. Another storm, later that same season, would have finally crippled the team but A.B. Turnbull, general manager of the *Green Bay Press Gazette*, came to the rescue. He stepped in and organized the businessmen of Green Bay to support the team, and the Green bay Football Company was formed — the beginning of the modern-day Community Corporation.

The Packers' saga, always eventful, spans some 67 years, but it was during the 'Lombardi era' that they showed their true colours. Former New York Giant Vince Lombardi signed with the Packers, as head coach, in 1959. In his first season he was voted Coach of the Year and in 1960 the Packers seized the Western Divisional title. Under his leadership they stormed on to take the World Championships in 1961, 1962, 1965, 1966 and 1967. Over nine years the team chalked up an astonishing 141 victories against 39 losses and four ties, for a remarkable 0.783 winning percentage. In 10 Division play-offs and World

Green Bay Packers vs NFL

	Won	Lost	Tied
Atlanta	8	6	0
Buffalo	1	2	0
Chicago	55	70	6
Cincinnati	2	3	0
Cleveland	7	5	0
Dallas	8	5	0
Denver	1	3	0
Detroit	57	47	7
Houston	2	2	0
Indianapolis	18	13	1
Kansas City	1	1	1
Los Angeles Raiders	1	4	0
Los Angeles Rams	34	39	2
Miami	0	4	0
Minnesota	24	24	1
New England	1	2	0
New Orleans	10	2	0
New York Giants	25	18	2
New York Jets	1	4	0
Philadelphia	17	5	0
Pittsburgh	16	10	0
San Diego	3	1	0
San Francisco	22	20	1
St Louis	38	21	4
Seattle	3	1	0
Tampa Bay	8	6	1
Washington	14	11	1

Championship games the Packers surged to victory nine times.
   Lombardi was a difficult act to follow and it wasn't until 1974 that the Packers again found a coach of similar calibre.
   'The prayers and patience of Packer fans everywhere...' was

End-of-season depth chart

OFFENSE

WR	— 80 James Lofton, 87 Walter Stanley
OLT	— 75 Ken Ruettgers
OLG	— 57 Rich Moran, 61 Blake Wingle
C	— 58 Mark Cannon, 60 Blake Moore, 57 Rich Moran
ORG	— 65 Ron Hallstrom, 68 Greg Koch
ORT	— 68 Greg Koch, 65 Ron Hallstrom
TE	— 82 Paul Coffman, 86 Ed West, 89 Mark Lewis
WR	— 85 Phillip Epps, 88 Preston Dennard
QB	— 18 Jim Zorn, 12 Lynn Dickey, 16 Randy Wright, 5 Vince Ferragamo
RB	— 40 Eddie Lee Ivery, 31 Gerry Ellis, 42 Gary Ellerson
RB	— 33 Jessie Clark, 31 Gerry Ellis

DEFENSE

DLE	— 76 Alphonso Carreker, 93 Robert Brown, 77 Mike Butler
NT	— 79 Donnie Humphrey, 94 Charles Martin
DRE	— 90 Ezra Johnson, 93 Robert Brown
LOLB	— 59 John Anderson, 51 Guy Prather
LILB	— 55 Randy Scott, 99 John Dorsey
RILB	— 91 Brian Noble, 52 George Cumby
ROLB	— 53 Mike Douglass, 51 Guy Prather
LCB	— 22 Mark Lee, 27 Gary Hayes
RCB	— 26 Tim Lewis, 23 Chuck Clanton
SS	— 37 Mark Murphy, 24 Mossy Cade
FS	— 41 Tom Flynn, 29 Ken Stills

SPECIAL TEAMS

P	— 17 Don Bracken
K	— 10 Al Del Greco
H	— 18 Jim Zorn
PR	— 85 Phillip Epps, 27 Gary Hayes, 87 Walter Stanley
KR	— 31 Gerry Ellis, 42 Gary Ellerson
LSN	— 58 Mark Cannon, 60 Blake Moore

ALSO WITH THE GREEN BAY PACKERS
39 Ronnie Burgess (DB), 25 Harlan Huckleby (RB), 74 Tim Huffman (G), 43 Daryll Jones (DB), 63 Terry Jones (NT), 28 Mike McLeod (DB), 35 Del Rodgers (RB), 67 Karl Swanke (T), 70 Keith Uecker (G), 46 Ralph Williams (WR), 50 Rich Wingo (LB)

the plea from Bart Starr when he took over the position of the Packers' head coach. He went on to say 'We will earn everything else', and he was right. From a disappointing 4-10 record in the first season, under Starr the Packers once again surged forward, and in 1978 they posted a winning record of 8-7-1. Their resurgence continued, despite setbacks and injuries, and in 1982 the Packers qualified for the play-offs. But a year later their fortunes once again plummeted.

On 24 December 1984, Starr was replaced by a former team-mate Forrest Greig. On taking over Greig declared, 'I took this job to field a winning team... that *will* happen.' Such determination and confidence paid dividends; from a 1-7 start in the 1984 season, the Packers made a convincing rebound to win seven of their last eight games. In 1984 in a mediocre season the Packers won eight and lost eight.

Last season

It was the same old story for the Packers: a slow start followed by a late winning run to finish 8-8 (the third time in four years they have achieved this dubious distinction).

But the Packers still have a masterly passing attack that centres on gifted receiver James Lofton, who set a new Packer record in 1985 gaining 8,816 receiving yards in a career, breaking a Packer record that had stood since 1945. Supported by fellow wide-out Philip Epps and tight end Paul Coffman, Loften provided a threat to the best defences, as he latched on to passes thrown by Lynn Dickey and Jim Zorn.

Quarterback is another area that coach Forrest Greig looked hard at last year. He expressed reservations about Lynn Dickey, but Zorn also failed to take his chance with 794 yards, 4 touchdowns and 6 interceptions. The defense is little more than adequate, although a line backing unit which stars Mike Douglas has been known to terrify a few offenses! Step forward the Tampa Bay Buccaneers who were held by the Green Bay defense to 65 net yards on Sunday 1 December when they were shut out 21-0. It was Green Bay's best defensive performance since 1 October 1967 when they held the Atlanta Falcons to 58 yards in a 23-0 victory at Milwaukee County Stadium. The shut-out of the Buccaneers was the first by the Packers since 23

131

October 1977 when they also blanked Tampa Bay 13-0.

Prediction

I've always had a soft spot for the Packers. But if they can finish well as they did last season then they should also be able to start well. I live in hope.

Play-off prediction

5

Los Angeles Rams

NATIONAL FOOTBALL CONFERENCE — WESTERN DIVISION

Address:	2327 West Lincoln Avenue, Anaheim, California 92801
Telephone:	(714) 535-7267 or (213) 585-5400
Colours:	Royal blue, gold and white
Stadium:	Anaheim Stadium, 1900 State College Boulevard, Anaheim, California 92806
Capacity:	69,007
Playing surface:	Grass

History

Forty million fans have packed the stadium and cheered on the LA Rams since their move to California from the less congenial climate of Cleveland, Ohio — they were the first team to move west.

It was 1946, World War Two was over; the GIs were coming home; and America began to thrive again. This new-found prosperity was especially evident in Los Angeles which quickly grew into a sprawling metropolis. Maxwell Styles of the Rams wrote that 'In moving our club to LA, we have given the game of Football one of its greatest stimulants in its history,' and went on to add: 'We are the first major league club in any sport to have established a permanent home on the great Pacific coast.'

Within six seasons the Rams won the World Championship, the first for Los Angeles, in beating the Cleveland Browns in

1951 — the score 24-17. The early 1950s were lean years for the Rams, but they were building, and under the guidance of Sid Gillman, the ex-head coach from the University of Cincinnati, in 1955 they advanced to the Conference title but were beaten by Cleveland. (By the way, if you ever wondered what the NFL Commissioner Peach Rozell did before he was the big cheese, he was at one time the Rams' publicist and in 1957 became their General Manager.) The year 1955 was a bad one: the team finished the season with a 2-10 record, the worst since 1937. It was not until 1967 that the Rams started showing some winning ways. They finished with an 11-1-2 league record to win the Coastal Division Championship, but went on to lose the Western Conference Championship game to the mighty Green Bay Packers.

In 1968, the Rams' defense set a new NFL fourteen-game record with fewest yards allowed, but it was in 1973 under the new direction of Chuck Knox that the team had its best year with a 12-2 season — they won the NFC West title — but lost in the play-offs to Dallas.

The next year they were in the play-offs only to lose to the Vikings in the NFL title game.

Building all the time, the Rams finally cracked it in 1979 when, despite a string of injuries, they finally made it to Superbowl XIV. They lost to the Steelers 31-19. In 1980 they moved to Anaheim — they got to the play-offs but lost to Dallas in the Wild Card.

Things started to go well for the Rams in 1983 when new coach John Robinson came and changed the whole pack of cards — one of those cards was an ace — Eric Dickerson was drafted as a Ram that year. They entered the play-offs as the Wild Card team before losing to the Redskins in Washington — but Dickerson was already showing that he was a superstar. He broke the NFL rookie rushing record with 1,808 yards and set five new Rams records in the process. The NFC Coach of the Year award went to John Robinson. The following year, 1984, they made the play-offs but lost to the Giants in the NFC Wild Card. But again Dickerson was showing his astonishing ability, beating O.J. Simpson's NFL record of 2,003 yards. 'It had to go some day,' said the Juice. 'I'm really glad it went to such a nice guy.'

134

Los Angeles Rams vs NFL

	Won	Lost	Tied
Atlanta	28	8	2
Buffalo	3	1	0
Chicago	27	43	3
Cincinnati	2	3	0
Cleveland	7	8	0
Dallas	10	10	0
Denver	3	2	0
Detroit	36	34	1
Green Bay	39	34	2
Houston	3	1	0
Indianapolis	14	20	2
Kansas City	3	0	0
Los Angeles Raiders	1	4	0
Miami	1	3	0
Minnesota	12	15	2
New England	1	2	0
New Orleans	23	9	0
New York Giants	16	8	0
New York Jets	2	2	0
Philadelphia	15	9	1
Pittsburgh	12	4	2
San Diego	2	1	0
San Francisco	44	26	2
St Louis	20	15	2
Seattle	3	0	0
Tampa Bay	5	2	0
Washington	5	14	1

Last season

The Rams, under the careful coaching of John Robinson, have become regulars in the play-off competition, but never really

135

End-of-season depth chart

OFFENSE

WR	— 80 Henry Ellard, 88 Michael Young
OLT	— 75 Irv Pankey, 62 Bill Bain
OLG	— 72 Kent Hill, 73 Russ Bolinger
C	— 61 Tony Slaton, 73 Russ Bolinger
ORG	— 60 Dennis Harrah, 73 Russ Bolinger
ORT	— 78 Jackie Slater, 62 Bill Bain
TE	— 81 David Hill, 87 Tony Hunter
WR	— 89 Ron Brown, 82 Bobby Duckworth
QB	— 5 Dieter Brock, 9 Jeff Kemp, 8 Steve Dils
RB	— 29 Eric Dickerson, 30 Barry Redden, 33 Charles White
HB	— 87 Tony Hunter, 44 Mike Guman

DEFENSE

DLE	— 93 Doug Reed, 68 Dennis Harrison, 91 Kevin Greene
NT	— 70 Charles DeJurnett, 98 Shawn Miller, 69 Greg Meisner
DRE	— 71 Reggie Doss, 77 Gary Jeter
LOLB	— 58 Mel Owens, 91 Kevin Greene
LILB	— 55 Carl Ekern, 90 Ed Brady, 57 Jim Laughlin
RILB	— 50 Jim Collins, 59 Mark Jerue
ROLB	— 54 Mike Wilcher, 51 Norwood Vann
LCB	— 27 Gary Green, 25 Jerry Gray
RCB	— 47 LeRoy Irvin, 25 Jerry Gray
SS	— 21 Nolan Cromwell, 48 Tim Fox
FS	— 20 Johnnie Johnson, 22 Vince Newsome

SPECIAL TEAMS

P	— 3 Dale Hatcher
K	— 1 Mike Lansford, 3 Dale Hatcher
H	— 8 Steve Dils, 21 Noland Cromwell, 9 Jeff Kemp
PR	— 80 Henry Ellard, 20 Johnnie Johnson
KR	— 89 Ron Brown, 30 Barry Redden
LSN	— 90 Ed Brady

ALSO WITH THE LOS ANGELES RAMS
52 George Andrews (LB), 34 Danny Bradley (WR), 26 Eric Harris (CB), 38 Damone Johnson (TE), 79 Duval Love (G), 83 James McDonald (TE), 94 John Meyer (DE), 43 Mike Pleasant (CB), Chuck Scott (WR), 65 Mike Shiner (T), 56 Doug Smith (C)

look capable of reaching the Superbowl. Though they have an outstanding offensive line and a superb blocking tight end in David Hill, and Eric Dickeson gains yards at a highly prodigious rate behind them, they have real quarterback problems. Last year Robinson brought in Dieter Brock, a 34-year-old with no previous NFL experience. He was not the answer and, as the season progressed, the passing game disappeared — much to the frustrations of wide out Henry Ellard and Tony Hunter. But rookie return man Ron Brown, the Olympic gold medallist sprinter, quickly established himself as the league's premier return man.

A no-nonsense defense could, on occasions, be compared with the best. But you don't win Superbowls with suspect quarterbacks, as the Rams found when they ran into Chicago.

Prediction

John Robinson is a great coach and although Dieter Brock had a baptism of fire last season, he did on occasions show great promise. If Dickeson stays healthy and their opponents make the mistake of kicking to Ron Brown, the Rams have every chance of success this season.

Play-off prediction

8

Minnesota Vikings

NATIONAL FOOTBALL CONFERENCE — CENTRAL DIVISION

Address:	9520 Viking Drive, Eden Prairie, Minnesota 55344
Telephone:	(612) 828-6500
Colours:	Purple, gold and white
Stadium:	Hubert H. Humphrey Metrodome, 500 11th Avenue, So. Minneapolis, Minnesota 55415
Capacity:	62,212
Playing surface:	SuperTurf

History

'They're not big... but they sure are slow.' That was how the Minnesota Vikings were described in 1961 — their team was made up of cast-offs and has-beens when they were first formed in 1960 and most pundits thought they didn't stand a chance of winning in their first season, but to everybody's surprise, including their own, they finished their first season with a fairly respectable 3-11 record.

By 1964 they had tied Green Bay for second place in the Western Conference with an 8-5-1. Their head coach Norm Van Brocklin, who had quarterbacked the Philadelphia Eagles, resigned in 1965 when their title hopes were dashed in a 41-21 hammering by Baltimore. Within a few hours he had changed his mind, but it led to a bad relationship with his players, especially Francis Tarkenton, his quarterback. During the 1966

139

season coach and quarterback hardly spoke to each other, and in 1967 Tarkenton issued a statement to the press, saying either he went or the coach went... he went. That was on 9 February and two days later Van Brocklin resigned; this time he didn't change his mind. Bud Grant came in as head coach and a new gifted quarterback from the Canadian league, Joe Knapp.

By 1968 the Vikings were beginning to look like a team again and they took their first Central Division Championship that year.

1969/70 was their season. They advanced to Superbowl IV — but they lost to the Chiefs 23-7. The following season, Knapp sat out the early games over a contract dispute before leaving for the Boston Patriots.

In 1973, helped by a good draft, the Vikings won their second Championship by beating Dallas 27-10. But in Superbowl VIII the Vikings were no match for Don Shula's Dolphins and were humiliated 24-7. Despite the loss, the following year they were back in Superbowl... but once again they lost... this time to Pittsburgh 16-6. These two consecutive defeats seemed to galvanize the team, and in 1976 the Vikings won their eighth Central Division title in nine years, but in their fourth Superbowl they were once again defeated by the Oakland Raiders 32-14; and in doing so Bud Grant, their coach, tied with Don Shula for the NFL record for most games as the losing coach of a Superbowl team. They finished the 1979 season 7-9, their first losing season since 1967.

In 1980 they clinched the NFC Central with a win against Cleveland but lost to the Eagles in the Division play-offs.

Their 1984 record was a dismal 3-13.

Last season

When the Vikings dumped the 49ers in the season's opener, we all wondered whether Bud Grant could really work a miracle? Well, in a sense he did, because he kept a team of only limited ability in play-off contention for much of the year before they ran out of gas. A running game was finally established, led by the rapier-like thrust of Darrin Nelson and the bulldozer charges of Ted Brown. And quarterback Tommy Kramer managed to keep injury-free and post his best season for some

Minnesota Vikings vs NFL

	Won	Lost	Tied
Atlanta	9	6	0
Buffalo	4	1	0
Chicago	25	22	2
Cincinnati	2	2	0
Cleveland	7	1	0
Dallas	5	10	0
Denver	2	2	0
Detroit	30	17	2
Green Bay	24	24	1
Houston	2	1	0
Indianapolis	5	12	1
Kansas City	2	2	0
Los Angeles Raiders	1	5	0
Los Angeles Rams	15	12	2
Miami	1	4	0
New England	1	2	0
New Orleans	8	4	0
New York Giants	6	1	0
New York Jets	1	3	0
Philadelphia	9	4	0
Pittsburgh	5	4	0
San Diego	3	3	0
San Francisco	13	12	1
St Louis	3	7	0
Seattle	1	2	0
Tampa Bay	11	5	0
Washington	5	4	0

years. Elsewhere Steve Jordan really blossomed, and Anthony Carter emerged as Kramer's big receiver.

Less impressive, however, was a defense which was particularly weak against the rush, a sharp-eyed secondary

141

End-of-season depth chart

OFFENSE

WR	— 89 Mike Jones, 88 Buster Rhymes, 87 Leo Lewis,
OLT	— 72 David Huffman, 68 Curtis Rouse
OLG	— 62 Brent Boyd, 71 Mark MacDonald
C	— 67 Dennis Swilley, 63 Kirk Lowdermilk, 51 Jim Hough
ORG	— 66 Terry Tausch, 71 Mark MacDonald
ORT	— 76 Tim Irwin, 72 David Huffman
TE	— 83 Steve Jordan, 86 Mike Mularkey, 84 Jay Carroll
WR	— 81 Anthony Carter, 85 Sammy White
QB	— 9 Tommy Kramer, 11 Wade Wilson, 13 Steve Bono
RB	— 46 Alfred Anderson, 23 Ted Brown
RB	— 20 Darrin Nelson, 36 Allen Rice

DEFENSE

DLE	— 79 Doug Martin, 74 Robert Smith, 73 Neil Elshire
NT	— 96 Tim Newton, 79 Doug Martin
DRE	— 75 Keith Millard, 77 Mark Mullaney
LOLB	— 56 Chris Doleman, 59 Matt Blair
LILB	— 50 Dennis Fowlkes, 99 David Howard
RILB	— 55 Scott Studwell, 99 David Howard
ROLB	— 57 Chris Martin, 99 David Howard
LCB	— 39 Carl Lee, 30 Issiac Holt, 27 John Turner
RCB	— 37 Willie Teal, 39 Carl Lee
SS	— 47 Joey Browner, 28 Ted Rosnagle
FS	— 27 John Turner, 49 Keith Nord

SPECIAL TEAMS

P	— 8 Greg Coleman
K	— 3 Jan Stenerud
H	— 8 Greg Coleman, 86 Mike Mularkey, 49 Keith Nord
PR	— 81 Anthony Carter, 20 Darrin Nelson, 87 Leo Lewis
KR	— 88 Buster Rhymes, 36 Allen Rice, 23 Ted Brown
LSN(P)	— 51 Jim Hough, 72 David Huffman
LSN(F)	— 51 Jim Hough, 63 Kirk Lowdermilk

ALSO WITH THE MINNESOTA VIKINGS
58 Walker Lee Ashley (LB), 21 Rufus Bess (CB), 64 Grant Feasel (T),
80 Jim Gustafson (WR), 61 Wes Hamilton (G), 53 Tim Meamber (LB),
35 Kyle Morrell (S), 38 Allanda Smith (DB)

inspired by Joey Browner and Rufus Bess kept opposing quarterbacks on their guard but the line and line backers failed to impress.

Prediction

Third in their Division behind the mighty Chicago and Green Bay, Minnesota finished on 7 and 9. If Bud Grant can kick that defense into some sort of shape and Kramer and Carter continue to improve, the Vikings could just about see post-season play.

Play-off prediction

5

New Orleans Saints

NATIONAL FOOTBALL CONFERENCE — WESTERN DIVISION

Address:	1500 Poydras Street, New Orleans, Louisiana 70112
Telephone:	(504) 522-1500
Colours:	Old gold, black, and white
Stadium:	Louisiana Superdome (*address as above*)
Capacity:	71,647
Playing surface:	AstroTurf

History

If it's a sin in the NFL never to have reached the play-offs or never to have had a winning season — then these Saints are sinners indeed. The team from the Superdome are the only NFL franchise never to have appeared in the play-offs and in 1979 and 1983 could only finish with records of 8-8, their best since they joined the NFL in 1967.

In their first year the Saints came marching in all right, with a pre-season record of 5-1, the best ever for a first-year team. Their fans were with them all the way in those early days, buying 20,000 season tickets the first day the box office opened. And in their first regular season game against the Rams, when a rookie John Gilliam returned the opening kick 94 yards for a touchdown, the 80,789 fans in Tulane Stadium thought not only the team but they too had been officially canonized. They were to be disappointed; the Rams came back to win 27-13.

The Saints, and New Orleans fans, had to wait for six more

145

games before they could record their first victory, beating the Eagles 31-24. In 1970 the team from New Orleans did enter the record books when Tommy Dempsey, a free-agent kicker, who was born without a right hand and without toes on his right foot, kicked the longest field goal in NFL history, an amazing 63 yards.

In 1972, some say in an effort to get closer to God, the Saints appointed a former astronaut as the club's executive vice-president. Richard Gordon, who had piloted Apollo XII to the moon, must have wished he had stayed in space, as the Saints ended the year with two wins, 11 losses and one tie, equalling their worst ever season.

1973, a new season — new Saints? No way. In the opening game they were humiliated by the Falcons 62-7 and the following week at Texas Stadium, God did not bother to look through the hole in the roof as the Cowboys killed the Saints 40-3. But then things changed . . . a bit. They won four of their next six games, including a surprising win over the Redskins to finish the season on 5-9, tying the best season the club had ever had.

It was the same story in 1974, 5-9; so would their luck change when they moved to the futuristic Superdome in 1975? On 28 September, in front of 52,531 fans in the first NFL game in the Superdome, the Saints didn't even score a point and went down 21-0 to Cincinnati. The following week their coach Joe North was fired.

In 1976 Hank Stram became the fourth coach in the club's ten-year history, and on 21 November the Saints tied a club record for most points scored in one game when they beat the Seahawks 51-27.

In 1978, quarterback Archie Manning was named Player of the Year, as the Saints ended the season 7-9, their best ever. Things were slightly better the following year, eight wins, eight losses.

But 1980 was their worst season, bringing an NFL record with 15 games lost in that sad campaign.

In 1984 the Saints' owner, John Mecom Jnr, announced that the Saints were for sale. Asking price — a *non-negotiable* $75 million. Tom Benson bought the Saints a few months later, at the bargain price of $70 million — now there is a Saint indeed!

New Orleans Saints vs NFL

	Won	Lost	Tied
Atlanta	11	23	0
Buffalo	1	2	0
Chicago	4	7	0
Cincinnati	2	3	0
Cleveland	1	8	0
Dallas	1	11	0
Denver	0	4	0
Detroit	4	4	1
Green Bay	2	10	0
Houston	2	2	1
Indianapolis	0	3	0
Kansas City	2	2	0
Los Angeles Raiders	0	3	1
Los Angeles Rams	9	23	0
Miami	1	3	0
Minnesota	4	8	0
New England	0	4	0
New York Giants	5	6	0
New York Jets	1	3	0
Philadelphia	6	8	0
Pittsburgh	4	4	0
San Diego	0	3	0
San Francisco	9	22	2
St Louis	4	9	0
Seattle	1	2	0
Tampa Bay	5	3	0
Washington	4	7	0

Last season

Yet another season of disappointment for coach 'Bum' Phillips
who gave up the game for good. Not that this will make life any
easier for the suffering Saints. They remain the only team never

End-of-season depth chart

OFFENSE

WR	— 88 Eugene Goodlow, 86 Jeff Groth
OLT	— 70 Jim Rourke, 77 Daren Gilbert, 64 Dave Lafary
OLG	— 63 Brad Edelman, 65 Adam Schreiber
C	— 60 Steve Korte, 61 Joel Hilgenberg
ORG	— 79 Ralph Williams, 65 Adam Schreiber
ORT	— 67 Stan Brock, 77 Daren Gilbert
TE	— 85 Hoby Brenner, 82 John Tice, 87 Larry Hardy
WR	— 84 Eric Martin, 19 Guido Merkens, 80 Mike Miller
QB	— 3 Bobby Hebert, 14 Richard Todd, 19 Guido Merkens
RB	— 35 Earl Campbell, 22 Tyrone Anthony
RB	— 30 Wayne Wilson, 43 Bobby Fowler

DEFENSE

DLE	— 75 Bruce Clark, 73 Frank Warren
NT	— 99 Tony Elliot, 74 Derland Moore
DRE	— 94 Jim Wilks, 97 James Geathers
LOLB	— 57 Rickey Jackson, 92 James Haynes
LILB	— 58 Glenn Redd, 54 Alvin Toles
RILB	— 50 Jack Del Rio, 55 Joe Kohlbrand
ROLB	— 92 James Haynes, 51 Whitney Paul, 55 Joe Kohlbrand
LCB	— 44 Dave Waymer, 26 Willie Tullis, 21 Earl Johnson
RCB	— 25 Johnnie Poe, 26 Willie Tullis, 21 Earl Johnson
SS	— 24 Terry Hoage, 39 Brett Maxie
FS	— 49 Frank Wattelet, 39 Brett Maxie

SPECIAL TEAMS

P	— 10 Brian Hansen
K	— 7 Morten Andersen
H	— 19 Guido Merkens
PR	— 26 Willie Tullis, 84 Eric Martin
KR	— 26 Willie Tullis, 22 Tyrone Anthony, 84 Eric Martin
LSN	— 61 Joel Hilgenberg, 60 Steve Korte

ALSO WITH THE NEW ORLEANS SAINTS

37 Rob Bennett (TE), 68 Kelvin Clark (G), 46 Hokie Gajan (RB), 20 Russel Gary (S), 66 Louis Oubre (G), 53 Scott Pelluer (LB), 71 Petey Perot (G), 47 David Rackley (CB), 83 Carl Roaches (WR), 18 David Wilson (QB), 89 Tyrone Young (WR)

to have made the play-offs and they never looked like threatening last year.

Quarterback Dave Wilson might be pleased with his own performance in his first full year, but he was badly let down by a line that leaked sacks like a colander. The leaky line meant that a passing game was difficult to establish and it was the same story on the run.

Traditionally the Saints are a defensive powerhouse, but last year they failed to live up to that billing: only Dave Waymer and Johnnie Poe in the secondary had any real impact. They alone provided a ray of light in the gloom surrounding the Superdome.

Prediction

Don't expect the Saints to come marching in this season. And don't expect them to join the club of 27. Still, the draft should help them a fair amount and it will be interesting to see if Bum Phillips' son, Wade, can do anything to improve matters.

Play-off Prediction

0

New York Giants

NATIONAL FOOTBALL CONFERENCE — EASTERN DIVISION

Address:	Giants Stadium, East Rutherford, New Jersey 07073
Telephone:	(201) 935-8111
Colours:	Blue, red, and white
Stadium:	Giants Stadium (*address as above*)
Capacity:	76,891
Playing surface:	AstroTurf

History

The luck of an Irishman, and a 'ghost' from Illinois; that's the unlikely combination that started the New York Giants.

It was 1925, and New Yorkers used to baseball heroes like Babe Ruth and fighters like Jack Dempsey, had not heard of pro football, let alone seen it. But the National Football League desperately needed a team in the nation's financial centre, and a plucky Irishman called Timothy J. Mara gave New York the Giants. He purchased the New York franchise for $2,500 but his main problem was to get New Yorkers to go and see the Giants. He tried to sign the 'Galloping Ghost' from Illinois, Red Grange, but Grange had already committed himself to the Bears, so Mara arranged a game in New York between his Giants and the Bears. New Yorkers keen to see the renowned Grange swarmed to the Giants' home, the Polo Grounds, and although the Giants lost, 70,000 New Yorkers watched — and pro football had come to the Big Apple.

151

Mara and the Giants struggled through the lean times, just managing to keep the franchise financially alive. From 1925 to 1955 the Giants played at the Polo Grounds and won three World Championships, and were NFL Eastern Champions nine times. In 1956 the Giants moved to Yankee Stadium, and they were growing all the time — 43,000 people turned out to their first home game against the Steelers on 21 October, and they were not disappointed. The Giants romped home 38-10 (Frank Gifford now, of course, with ABC TV was in that game and scored a touchdown). That auspicious start led to the Giants' first NFL Championship since 1938. From 1956 to 1963 the Giants lost four Championship games, but coming so close they were building a loyal and dedicated following.

The season of 1973 was disastrous: 2-11-1; and three years later they moved to East Rutherford, New Jersey, to Giants Stadium. But they were still no match for their contemporaries, winning only three games in 14.

In 1979 a first-round draft choice, Phil Simms, took over at quarterback, but it was another sad year for the Giants who finished with a record of 6-10. The next year was even worse. Their defense allowed opponents to score a near-record 425 points, and the Giants finished 4-12.

In 1981 the Giants saw play-off action when they beat the Eagles in the Wild Card 27-21, but their hopes of going to their first Superbowl were dashed by the eventual Superbowl Champions, the San Francisco 49ers who beat them 38-24. However, they'd made it to the play-offs, and it was a sign that things were changing.

On 23 December 1984, in front of 67,000 people at Anaheim Stadium, New York went to LA and the Giants beat the Rams 16-13. But six days later, at Candlestick Park, despite the Giants' defense intercepting Joe Montana three times and sacking him four times for 28 yards, the Giants fell to the 49ers 21-10.

Last season

The Giants confirmed their status as a dangerous side with a second consecutive visit to the play-offs. Quarterback Phil Simms must now rate as one of the top five in his position, while

New York Giants vs NFL

	Won	Lost	Tied
Atlanta	5	6	0
Buffalo	2	1	0
Chicago	16	27	2
Cincinnati	0	3	0
Cleveland	16	26	2
Dallas	13	32	2
Denver	1	2	0
Detroit	11	18	1
Green Bay	18	25	2
Houston	3	0	0
Indianapolis	3	7	0
Kansas City	4	1	0
Los Angeles Raiders	0	3	0
Los Angeles Rams	8	16	0
Miami	0	1	0
Minnesota	1	6	0
New England	1	1	0
New Orleans	6	5	0
New York Jets	2	2	0
Philadelphia	56	45	2
Pittsburgh	41	26	3
San Diego	2	2	0
San Francisco	10	7	0
St Louis	53	31	2
Seattle	3	1	0
Tampa Bay	6	3	0
Washington	58	46	3

pint-sized Joe Morris proved that you don't have to be a giant to play for the Giants. But while Morris led the rushing game, Simms threw to a variety of receivers, including rookie Mark Bavaro who looked excellent.

153

End-of-season depth chart

OFFENSE

WR	—	88 Bob Johnson, 87 Byron Williams
OLT	—	60 Brad Benson, 72 Gordon King
OLG	—	67 Billy Ard, 69 David Jordan
C	—	65 Bart Oates, 62 Conrad Goode
ORG	—	61 Chris Godfrey, 69 David Jordan, 72 Gordon King
ORT	—	63 Karl Nelson, 72 Gordon King
TE	—	89 Mark Bavaro, 85 Don Hasselbeck
WR	—	86 Lionel Manuel, 80 Phil McConkey, 81 Stacy Robinson
QB	—	11 Phil Simms, 17 Jeff Rutledge
RB	—	20 Joe Morris, 33 George Adams, 22 Lee Rouson
RB	—	26 Rob Carpenter, 44 Maurice Carthon, 30 Tony Galbreath

DEFENSE

DLE	—	76 Curtis McGriff, 75 George Martin
NT	—	64 Jim Burt, 78 Jerome Sally
DRE	—	70 Leonard Marshall, 79 Dee Hardison, 71 Casey Merrill
LOLB	—	57 Byron Hunt, 58 Carl Banks, 54 Andy Headen
LILB	—	55 Gary Reasons, 51 Robbie Jones
RILB	—	53 Harry Carson, 51 Robbie Jones
ROLB	—	56 Lawrence Taylor, 54 Andy Headen
LCB	—	34 Elvis Patterson, 21 Ted Watts
RCB	—	23 Perry Williams, 27 Herb Welch
SS	—	48 Kenny Hill, 21 Ted Watts, 27 Herb Welch
FS	—	43 Terry Kinard, 27 Herb Welch

SPECIAL TEAMS

P	—	5 Sean Landeta
K	—	3 Eric Schubert
H	—	17 Jeff Rutledge, 80 Phil McConkey
PR	—	80 Phil McConkey
KR	—	80 Phil McConkey, 33 George Adams, 30 Tony Galbreath
LSN	—	65 Bart Oates, 62 Conrad Goode

ALSO WITH THE NEW YORK GIANTS

73 Kerin Belcher (C), 29 Bill Currier (S), 24 Kenny Daniel (CB), 39 Tyrone Davis (CB), 6 Ali Haji-Sheikh (K), 36 Mark Haynes (CB), 15 Jeff Hostetler (QB), 77 Damien Johnson (T), Brian Johnston (C), 82 Vyto Kalo (TE), 84 Zeke Mowatt (TE), 66 Bill Roberts (T), 38 John Tuggle (RB), 28 Larry Winters (DB)

There are no glaring weaknesses on defense, either. The pass rushing unit has earned respect, while Lawrence Taylor leads a group of linebackers who must rank as the NFL's strongest in terms of depth. But there is a problem at place kicker, where Ali Haji-Sheik was injured and replacement Eric Schubert lacked consistency.

Prediction

Coach Bill Parcells will sort out his problems this summer and if he is successful the Giants could be on the verge of something very big *this* season. The Giants have a lot going for them. Watch them win the NFC East.

Play-off prediction

10

Philadelphia Eagles

NATIONAL FOOTBALL CONFERENCE — EASTERN DIVISION

Address: Veterans Stadium, Broad Street and
Pattison Avenue, Philadelphia,
Pennsylvania 19148

Telephone: (215) 463-2500

Colours: 'Kelly' green, silver and white

Stadium: Veterans Stadium (*address as above*)

Capacity: 71,640

Playing surface: AstroTurf

History

In the early 1930s no sport could be played in Philadelphia on Sunday — it was a state law. But in 1933, with that law about to be repealed, Bert Bell and Lud Wray bought an NFL franchise for $2,500. The team was named the Eagles and in their first Sunday game in 1933 against the Bears at Baker Bowl they scored a 3-3 tie. In 1943 the Eagles briefly merged with the Pittsburgh Steelers. This strange marriage resulted in the team being called 'The Steagles'. The marriage was dissolved at the end of the season!

In 1944, in the first round of the college draft, the Eagles selected a half back called Steve Van Buren and by 1945 he led the NFL with 832 rushing yards and 110 points scored. After second places for three consecutive years — 1944, 1945 and 1946 — 1948 brought victory. The Eagles stormed the Chicago Cardinals in a blinding snow blizzard at Shibe Park. Van Buren nearly didn't make the match at all. On the morning of the game he'd woken up, seen the snow and assumed the match would be postponed. But the game was on, and, alerted by a call from the coach Earle (Greasy) Neil, Van Burch leapt into a trolley car, crossed town to the Stadium and went on to score the game's only touchdown! The team finished the season with an overall record of 10-2-1. In 1949 the Eagles were sold for $250,000 — it proved to be a victorious year with the team winning their third straight Eastern Division title, and defending their NFL Championship with a convincing 14-0 win over the Los Angeles Rams. Their overall record was 12-1.

The year 1952 was one of change for the Eagles. Van Buren suffered a serious knee injury in training camp and retired, while Jim Trimble was named the new head coach. Trimble was looking for a quarterback and found Bobby Thomason from Green Bay and, by tightening his defense, the Eagles won seven games and tied the New York Giants for second place with a 7-5 record.

The 1960s saw the retirement of the league's most valuable player, Van Brocklin, who was an astonishingly accurate quarterback. At the same time as he left, the club sustained an unprecedented number of injuries and in 1962 they sank to last place. But, by the second half of the decade, the Eagles were soaring back. And in 1966, after extensive roster changes, they finished 9-5 — their first winning season for five years. By 1969 the Eagles were once again valuable, their franchise passing from Gerry Wolman to Leonard Tose, a man who had made a fortune in trucking. He also paid a fortune for the club, $16.1 million (at the time a record price for a professional sports team).

The move in 1971 to a new home at Veteran Stadium grounded the Eagles. Defeat followed defeat, and after a disastrous 2-11-1 1972 season the general manager resigned and the entire coaching staff were released. Under new coach Mike McCormack 1973 looked better — it certainly couldn't have been bleaker — with an exciting offensive season; wide receiver Harold Carmichael led the NFL with 67 pass receptions. But it wasn't until 1978 that the Eagles could fly again, just about, to record 9-7 — their first winning season since 1966. Wilbert Montgomery rushed for 1,220 yards — the first Eagle since Van

Philadelphia Eagles vs NFL

	Won	Lost	Tied
Atlanta	6	6	1
Buffalo	3	1	0
Chicago	4	19	1
Cincinnati	0	4	0
Cleveland	11	29	1
Dallas	17	34	0
Denver	3	1	0
Detroit	9	12	2
Green Bay	5	17	0
Houston	3	0	0
Indianapolis	5	5	0
Kansas City	1	0	0
Los Angeles Raiders	1	3	0
Los Angeles Rams	9	15	1
Miami	2	3	0
Minnesota	4	9	0
New England	3	2	0
New Orleans	8	6	0
New York Giants	45	56	2
New York Jets	3	0	0
Pittsburgh	42	25	3
San Diego	1	2	0
San Francisco	4	10	1
St Louis	34	40	4
Seattle	2	0	0
Tampa Bay	2	1	0
Washington	39	57	5

Buren to surpass 1,200 yards in a single season.

During the 1980 season the Eagles' defense worked hard, allowing fewer points (222) against them than any other league team. It was a record that stood them in very good stead on tie-

End-of-season depth chart

OFFENSE
WR   — 81 Kenny Jackson, 86 Gregg Garrity, 80 Keith Baker
OLT   — 66 Ken Reeves, 72 Kevin Allen
OLG   — 73 Steve Kenney, 67 Gerry Feehery
C   — 65 Mark Dennard, 67 Gerry Feehery
ORG   — 63 Ron Baker, 67 Gerry Feehery
ORT   — 74 Leonard Mitchell, 77 Tom Jelesky
TE   — 88 John Spagnola, 89 David Little, 84 John Goode
WR   — 82 Mike Quick, 86 Gregg Garrity, 80 Keith Baker
QB   — 7 Ron Jaworski, 12 Randall Gunningham
RB   — 41 Earnest Jackson, 36 Herman Hunter
RB   — 26 Michael Haddix, 39 Major Everett, 38 Jairo Penaranda

DEFENSE
DLE   — 91 Reggie White, 93 Thomas Strauthers, 94 Byron Darby
NT   — 71 Ken Clarke, 99 Joe Drake
DRE   — 98 Greg Brown, 93 Thomas Strauthers, 94 Byron Darby
LOLB — 51 Reggie Wilkes, 52 Rich Kraynak
LILB   — 55 Mike Reichenbach, 52 Rich Kraynak, 53 Dwayne Jiles
RILB   — 58 Anthony Griggs, 52 Rich Kraynak, 53 Dwayne Jiles
ROLB — 50 Garry Cobb, 52 Rich Kraynak, 59 Joel Williams
LCB   — 43 Roynell Young, 29 Elbert Foules, 21 Evan Cooper
RCB   — 46 Herman Edwards, 29 Elbert Foules, 20 Andre Waters
SS   — 24 Ray Ellis, 22 Brenard Wilson
FS   — 48 Wes Hopkins, 22 Brenard Wilson

SPECIAL TEAMS
P   — 2 Michael Horan
K   — 8 Paul McFadden
H   — 12 Randall Cunningham, 2 Michael Horan
PR   — 21 Evan Cooper, 20 Andre Waters
KR   — 36 Herman Hunter, 20 Andre Waters
LSN   — 65 Mark Dennard, 67 Gerry Feehery

ALSO WITH THE PHILADELPHIA EAGLES
85 Ron Johnson (WR), 54 Jon Kimmel (LB), 69 Dwaine
Morris (NT), 76 Greg Naron (G), 57 Tom Polley (LB), 95 Jody Schulz (LB),
83 Tony Woodruff (WR)

breaking procedures and won them the NFC title. A year later, the Eagles' defense once again proved to be their strength, giving up only 221 points. They seemed to be once again heading for the clouds, building a 10-6 record and taking second place in the NFC East. But in a Wild Card game the New York Giants pounced and won 27-21.

In 1984 the Eagles excited the crowd at Veteran Stadium by winning five out of eight matches, compared to a meagre one in eight in 1983. There was at last something to cheer about. They finished the 1984 season with a record of six wins, nine losses and one tie.

Last season

At one stage, the Eagles looked capable of causing some real surprises. A highly motivated quarterback Ron Jaworski started to play to his true potential, finishing the season with 3,390 yards and 17 touchdowns, and ex-Charger Ernest Jackson began to grind them on the ground. And with wide out Mike Quick and T.E. John Spagnola catching everything that was thrown their way, anything seemed possible. Sadly for the Eagles (and coach Marion Campbell who lost his job), they were unable to mount a sustained challenge.

On defense, safety Wes Hopkins had the kind of year you dream about and was rightly named to the ProBowl. He was the inspiration behind the secondary which shut off most aerial attacks. But it was a different story up front, where a lack of penetration was cruelly exposed on several occasions.

Prediction

Last season's record of 7 and 9 could well be bettered this year. Post-season play is something the Eagles could only dream about, but then, some dreams do come true...

Play-off prediction

4

St Louis Cardinals

NATIONAL FOOTBALL CONFERENCE — EASTERN DIVISION

Address: Busch Stadium, Box 888, St Louis,
                    Missouri 63188

Telephone: (314) 421-0777

Colours: Cardinal red, black and white

Stadium: Busch Stadium, 200 Stadium Plaza, St
                    Louis, Missouri 63102

Capacity: 51,392

Playing surface: AstroTurf

History

When, in 1898, a poor south-side Chicago football team bought
the faded maroon jerseys of the famed University of Chicago,
they bought more than they bargained for. Proud Father Chris
O'Brien when taunted, snapped: 'That's not maroon, it's
cardinal red.' The St. Louis Cardinals had bought themselves an
identity! The team thrived, and in 1920 was one of the original
11 Charter members of the American Professional Football
League. Five years later, the league had expanded to include 20
teams and the Cardinals won their first NFL title. In 1929 the
Cardinals were bought by dentist Dr David Jones who, in turn,
sold them to Charles W. Bidwill — father of the present owner.
The 1930s and much of the 1940s were difficult times, to say the
least. However, in 1947 things began to change. The Cardinals
won the Western Divisional title and felled the Philadelphia
Eagles 28-21 for the NFL Championship.

163

Moving from Chicago to St Louis in 1960, the Cardinals ravaged the Rams in a 43-21 season opener, finishing fourth with a 6-5-1 record. Fourteen years later they captured the NFC Eastern Division Championship and went to the play-offs with a convincing 10-4 record — only to be vanquished by marauding Vikings 30-14. The following year, 1975, brought another Divisional title and another play-off loss — this time to the Rams who revelled in their 35-23 victory.

In the 1982 campaign they saw play-off action but were crushed by Green Bay, 41-16. Under coach Jim Hamifan they finished the 1984 season with a record of nine wins and seven losses.

Last season

Just about everything that could go wrong did for St Louis in 1985. Key players such as Roy Greene, quarterback Neil Lomax, and running back Ottis Anderson, spent varying amounts of time on injured reserve. A hopeful start turned quickly to disappointment and ultimately disaster, propping up the NFC East with a dismal five wins, 11 losses.

As results started to go against them, morale began to plummet. The offense spluttered all year, despite the excellent performances of Stump Mitchell and Pat Tilley. And the defense achieved very little in terms of penetration. Even special teams were a flop as kickers came and went. By the end, owner Jim Bidwill had had enough, and fired coach Jim Hamifan and his entire staff. Then a drugs problem appeared, and an angry Bidwill started talking about uprooting the franchise to Phoenix. At the time of writing, this is a franchise in turmoil.

Prediction

With so many problems, it'll take a miracle to make it all happen.

Play-off prediction

0

St Louis Cardinals vs NFL

	Won	Lost	Tied
Atlanta	6	3	0
Buffalo	3	1	0
Chicago	25	50	6
Cincinnati	1	2	0
Cleveland	10	30	3
Dallas	17	29	1
Denver	0	1	1
Detroit	15	25	5
Green Bay	21	38	4
Houston	3	1	0
Indianapolis	5	4	0
Kansas City	0	3	1
Los Angeles Raiders	1	1	0
Los Angeles Rams	15	20	2
Miami	0	5	0
Minnesota	7	3	0
New England	4	1	0
New Orleans	9	4	0
New York Giants	31	53	2
New York Jets	2	1	0
Philadelphia	40	34	4
Pittsburgh	20	29	3
San Diego	1	2	0
San Francisco	7	6	0
Seattle	2	0	0
Tampa Bay	1	3	0
Washington	32	49	2

End-of-season depth chart

OFFENSE

WR	—	81 Roy Green, 84 J.T. Smith, 86 Clyde Duncan
OLT	—	67 Luis Sharpe, 56 Carlos Scott
OLG	—	66 Doug Dawson, 61 Lance Smith
C	—	64 Randy Clark, 56 Carlos Scott
ORG	—	71 Joe Bostic, 61 Lance Smith
ORT	—	63 Tootie Robbins, 61 Lance Smith
TE	—	80 Doug Marsh, 89 Greg LaFleur
WR	—	83 Pat Tilley, 87 Earnest Gray, 28 Jay Novacek
QB	—	15 Neil Lomax, 12 Scott Brunner, 14 Rick McIvor
RB	—	30 Stump Mitchell, 32 Ottis Anderson, Tony Mumford
RB	—	24 Ron Wolfley, 40 Randy Love

DEFENSE

DLE	—	60 Al Baker, 76 Stafford Mays
DLT	—	73 Mark Duda, 74 Scott Bergold
DRT	—	65 David Galloway, 74 Scott Bergold
DRE	—	75 Curtis Greer, 76 Stafford Mays
LLB	—	57 Niko Noga, 52 Charlie Baker
MLB	—	54 E.J. Junior, 55 Danny Spradlin
RLB	—	53 Freddie Joe Nunn, 50 Bob Harris
LCB	—	48 Lionel Washington, 47 Cedric Mack, 35 Jeff Griffen
RCB	—	44 Wayne Smith, 42 Bobby Johnson
SS	—	45 Leonard Smith, 38 Lee Nelson
FS	—	43 Lonnie Young, 38 Lee Nelson

SPECIAL TEAMS

P	—	18 Carl Birdsong
K	—	11 Novo Bojovic
H	—	18 Carl Birdsong
PR	—	84 J.T. Smith, 30 Stump Mitchell
KR	—	30 Stump Mitchell, 40 Randy Love
LSN	—	64 Randy Clark, 56 Carlos Scott

ALSO WITH THE ST LOUIS CARDINALS
31 Earl Ferrell (RB), 78 Elois Grooms (DT), 36 Perry Harrington (RB),
59 Thomas Howard (LB), 51 Rob Monaco (C), 23 Benny Perrin (S),
72 Dan Ralph (DT), 33 Quentin Walker (WR)

166

San Francisco 49ers

NATIONAL FOOTBALL CONFERENCE — WESTERN DIVISION

Address:	711 Nevada Street, Redwood City, California 94061
Telephone:	(415) 365-3420
Colours:	49ers gold and scarlet
Stadium:	Candlestick Park, San Francisco, California 94124
Capacity:	61,413
Playing surface:	Grass

History

In 1950 the 49ers were flat on their faces! They'd won just three games in their NFL debut season. Perhaps it was a rival coach's comment that the San Francisco 49ers were 'just not big enough or tough enough' which spurred them on to an amazing reversal of form, because by 1951 they'd pulled themselves up by their bootlaces and finished third in the NFL National Conference. In 1953 with Bob St Claire, all 6ft 9in and 260lbs of him, as part of the squad, the 49ers had their best season to date in the NFL, losing only three games with a total of nine points.

The season of 1957 was a dramatic one for the 49ers and a creative one in which they developed the 'Alley-oop pass'. Huge crowds flocked to see them play matches which proved time and again to be cliff-hangers. But feelings really ran high during a contest with the Chicago Bears. Founder Tony Morabito suffered a fatal heart attack during half-time and the 49ers, who

167

had been trailing 17-7, fought for a great come-back victory of 21-17.

By 1958, the San Francisco 49ers were face down again, having been ravaged by the Rams 33-3 and 56-7. And 1959 proved unspectacular, while the 1960 season seemed hopeless when it opened. Desperate and direct action was needed, and that's just what the shot-gun formation provided. The 49ers were salvaged — they won four of their last five games and tied for second place in the Western Conference.

Outstanding offensive action during the 1963 season thrust the 49ers from bottom to fourth place in the Western Division as the team led the NFL in both scoring and total offense, their overall record 7-6-1.

The 1970s began with the greatest year ever for the club: their record was 10-3-1. Dick Nolan was named NFC Coach of the Year, John Brody Player of the Year and cornerback Bruce Taylor Rookie of the Year. By taking the NFC Western Division Championship, the 49ers had for the first time in their 25-year history grasped a title. During 1981 the 49ers clinched a whole fistful of firsts and bests. Their 16-3 record was the best in the league that year and fourth best in NFL history — it was certainly the best ever for the 49ers. They won the NFC Western Division title, the NFC Championship crown and the World Championship Superbowl XVI. Coach Bill Walsh was named NFC Coach of the Year and six 49ers, Dwight Clark, Randy Cross, Joe Montana, Fred Dean, Ronnie Lott, Dwight Hicks, were named for the Pro Bowl. By winning fifteen of their last sixteen games — beating five opponents twice — the 49ers became the second team to go from worst NFL record (2-14 in 1979) to the league best (13-3 in 1980) in just three seasons.

In 1983, for the second time in three seasons, San Francisco played in the NFC Championship game, and lost 24-21 to Washington in a game of high drama. The following year, 1984, the 49ers broke 14 team records on their way to winning Superbowl XIX, routing the Miami Dolphins 38-16. That year they were quite simply untouchable. Said Bill Walsh, 'This is the greatest football team and the greatest group of people I've had the pleasure to be associated with during my coaching career. Without a doubt this is the best team in football today.' Joe Montana, Wendell Tyler, Keith Fahnhorst, Randy Cross and

San Francisco 49ers vs NFL

	Won	Lost	Tied
Atlanta	21	17	0
Buffalo	1	2	0
Chicago	23	24	1
Cincinnati	4	1	0
Cleveland	4	8	0
Dallas	8	8	1
Denver	2	3	0
Detroit	23	26	1
Green Bay	20	22	1
Houston	3	2	0
Indianapolis	14	21	0
Kansas City	3	1	0
Los Angeles Raiders	2	3	0
Los Angeles Rams	26	44	2
Miami	1	4	0
Minnesota	12	13	1
New England	3	1	0
New Orleans	22	9	2
New York Giants	7	10	0
New York Jets	3	1	0
Philadelphia	10	4	1
Pittsburgh	6	6	0
San Diego	1	3	0
St Louis	6	7	0
Seattle	2	1	0
Tampa Bay	5	1	0
Washington	8	6	1

Fred Quillan on offense and Dwight Hicks, Ronnie Lott, Carlton Williamson and Eric Wright (the entire secondary) and Keena Turner on defense were selected to play in the Pro Bowl.

End-of-season depth chart

OFFENSE
WR   — 87 Dwight Clark, 85 Mike Wilson
OLT   — 77 Bubba Paris, 69 Bruce Collie
OLG   — 68 John Ayers, 69 Bruce Collie
C   — 56 Fred Quillan, 52 John Hill, 68 John Ayers
ORG   — 62 Guy McIntyre, 69 Bruce Collie
ORT   — 71 Keith Fahnhorst, 60 Vince Stroth
TE   — 81 Russ Francis, 86 John Frank
WR   — 80 Jerry Rice, 88 Freddie Solomon
QB   — 16 Joe Montana, 6 Matt Cavanaugh
RB   — 26 Wendell Tyler, 24 Derrick Harmon, 32 Carl Monroe
RB   — 33 Roger Craig, 30 Billy Ring

DEFENSE
DLE   — 75 John Harty, 72 Jeff Stover
NT   — 95 Michael Carter, 78 Manu Tuiasosopo
DRE   — 76 Dwaine Board, 79 Jim Stuckey, 74 Fred Dean
LOLB   — 90 Todd Shell, 53 Milt McColl
LILB   — 50 Riki Ellison, 55 Jim Fahnhorst
RILB   — 99 Michael Walter, 57 Jim Kovach
ROLB   — 58 Keena Turner, 54 Ron Ferrari
LCB   — 22 Dwight Hicks, 42 Ronnie Lott, 20 Tory Nixon
RCB   — 21 Eric Wright, 43 Dana McLemore
SS   — 27 Carlton Williamson, 49 Jeff Fuller
FS   — 42 Ronnie Lott, 22 Dwight Hicks

SPECIAL TEAMS
P   — 4 Max Runager
K   — 14 Ray Wersching
H   — 6 Matt Cavanaugh, 16 Joe Montana
PR   — 43 Dana McLemore, 24 Derrick Harmon
KR   — 32 Carl Monroe, 24 Derrick Harmon, 43 Dana McLemore
LSN   — 56 Fred Quillan, 68 John Ayers

ALSO WITH THE SAN FRANCISCO 49ERS
89 Earl Cooper (TE), 51 Randy Cross (G), 28 Tom Holmoe (S),
Charles Huff (DB), 97 Gary Johnson (NT), 66 Allan Kennedy (T), Fulton
Kuykendall, 83 Renaldo Nehemiah (WR), 61 Jesse Sapolu (G/C) John
Steevens (G/C)

Last season

The 49ers suffered a number of injuries during the 1985 campaign. They were also defending Champions, and as such were the team that all wanted to win. It was a combination of these factors that resulted in a patchy season and losses to the likes of Minnesota, Detroit and New Orleans. The magic of 1984 was just not there in 1985, although running back Roger Craig did achieve the unique distinction of becoming the first player to rush for and receive 1,000 yards. But however much Craig ran and rookie Jerry Rice scorched, and quarterback Joe Montana scrambled, the offense looked nearly mortal again.

And that goes for the defense, despite heroics from Keena Turner, Ronnie Lott and Dwaine Board. To make matters worse, veteran kicker Ray Wersching seems to be going off the boil as well. Though they achieved a play-off spot, the 49ers will look back at 1985 as the year of bitter disappointment.

Prediction

It was all a bit too much last season for the 49ers. But they still have all the ingredients to be Champions again. Last season's disappointment will certainly concentrate their minds.

Play-off prediction

9

Tampa Bay Buccaneers

NATIONAL FOOTBALL CONFERENCE — CENTRAL DIVISION

Address:	One Buccaneer Place, Tampa, Florida 33607
Telephone:	(813) 870-2700
Colours:	Florida orange, white and red
Stadium:	Tampa Stadium, North Dale Mabry, Tampa, Florida 33607
Capacity:	74,270
Playing surface:	Grass

History

Pro football came to Tampa Bay on 10 August 1968 when Washington met Atlanta in the newly-opened $14.1 million Tampa Stadium, but it was not until 24 April 1974 that Tampa Bay was awarded the 27th NFL franchise. It went to Hugh Culverhouse, a lawyer and real estate investor, and he paid a cool $16 million for the privilege. On 15 February 1975, after 400 nicknames had been suggested, it was announced that Tampa's team would be known as the Buccaneers, and two months later they unveiled their official colours of orange, white and red trim and the logo of the swashbuckling buccaneer.

It was not an auspicious start for the Bucks. In their first regular season game they were shut out 20-0 at Houston, and a week later in their first home game they were again shut out 23-0. The Bucks were far from swashbuckling! In their first year they didn't win a game, finishing with a 0-14 record, the first team to achieve that dubious distinction in NFL history. In their second (1977) season they only managed two wins out of fourteen games. The following year they improved marginally, with a 5-11 record. But the fortunes of the Bucks changed in 1977. By winning 17-13 at Chicago, they became the only unbeaten team in the NFL — that game proved decisive in the race for the NFC Central when Tampa tied with Chicago at 10-6 and won on the tie-breaker. On 29 December the Bucks defeated Philadelphia in a Divisional play-off game and they went through to the Conference title game, where they were shut out by the LA Rams 9-0.

In 1981 they won the NFC Central Division title, but were soundly beaten by Dallas 38-0. On 2 January 1983, the Buccaneers qualified for post-season play for the third time in four years with a dramatic 26-23 win over the Bears, but the following Sunday the Cowboys dominated 30-17, and eliminated them from the play-offs.

Although James Wilder excelled as a running back, in 1983 the Bucks could only manage a 2-14 season and by its close the Bucks looked burnt out. Eighteen of their players were on injured reserve.

In 1984 Tampa got a new quarterback from Denver in the shape of Steve De Berg. He certainly helped revitalize them as they ended the season third in the NFC Central with a record of 6-10.

Last season

One good thing came out of Tampa Bay's unhappy 2-14 season. They ended the campaign with the worst record in the NFL, and therefore earned first pick in the draft. And maybe this will help a team which really isn't as bad as its record suggests. Running back James Wilder is certainly one of the best. Wideout Kevin House and tight end Jimmie Giles both had seasons to be proud of, and quarterbacks Steve De Berg and Steve Young combined youth and experience. The defense badly missed its twin towers of support: Hugh Green (who was traded) and Lee Roy Selmon (who was sidelined through injury). Without them, the defense looked a little threadbare and conceded 448 points on the year (only Atlanta allowed more). But rookie kicker Donald

Tampa Bay Buccaneers vs NFL

	Won	Lost	Tied
Atlanta	3	2	0
Buffalo	2	1	0
Chicago	4	12	0
Cincinnati	1	2	0
Cleveland	0	3	0
Dallas	0	6	0
Denver	0	2	0
Detroit	7	9	0
Green Bay	6	8	1
Houston	1	2	0
Indianapolis	1	2	0
Kansas City	2	3	0
Los Angeles Raiders	0	2	0
Los Angeles Rams	2	5	0
Miami	1	2	0
Minnesota	5	11	0
New England	0	2	0
New Orleans	3	5	0
New York Giants	3	6	0
New York Jets	1	3	0
Philadelphia	1	2	0
Pittsburgh	0	3	0
San Diego	0	2	0
San Francisco	1	5	0
St Louis	3	1	0
Seattle	0	2	0
Washington	0	2	0

Igwebuike looked handy, and seemed to have a bright future ahead of him.

End-of-season depth chart

OFFENSE

WR   — 89 Kevin House, 83 Theo Bell
OLT — 66 George Yarno, 79 Ken Kaplan
OLG — 72 Steve Courson, 68 Rick Mallory, 64 Joe Shearin
C   — 60 Randy Grimes, 50 Steve Wilson
ORG — 62 Sean Farrell, 68 Rick Mallory
ORT — 73 Ron Heller, 79 Ken Kaplan
TE   — 88 Jimmie Giles, 85 Mark Witte
WR   — 87 Gerald Carter, 84 David Verser
QB   — 8 Steve Young, 17 Steve De Berg, 7 Alan Risher
RB   — 32 James Wilder, 20 Ron Springs, 38 George Peoples
HB   — 86 Calvin Magee, 80 K.D. Dunn, 40 Adger Armstrong

DEFENSE

DLE — 78 John Cannon, 71 Mark Studaway
NT   — 76 David Logan, 67 Karl Morgan
DRE — 90 Ron Holmes, 75 Chris Lindstrom
LOLB — 54 Ervin Randle, 57 Keith Browner
LILB — 58 Jeff Davis, 56 Cecil Johnson
RILB — 56 Cecil Johnson, 55 Dennis Johnson
ROLB — 51 Chris Washington, 54 Ervin Randle
LCB — 23 Jeremiah Castille, 26 Rickey Easmon
RCB — 21 John Holt, 26 Rickey Easmon
SS   — 30 David Greenwood, 31 Craig Curry, 24 Mike Prior
FS   — 44 Ivory Sully, 31 Craig Curry

SPECIAL TEAMS

P   — 5 Frank Garcia
K   — 1 Donald Igwebuike
H   — 7 Alan Risher, 17 Steve De Berg
PR   — 27 Mike Prior
KR   — 20 Ron Springs, 84 David Verser
LSN — 79 Ken Kaplan, 50 Steve Wilson

ALSO WITH THE TAMPA BAY BUCCANEERS
Corwyn Aldredge (TE), 82 Jerry Bell (TE), 52 Scot Brantley (LB),
29 Leon Bright (RB/KR), 81 Phil Freeman (WR), 65 Don Fielder (DE), 91 John
Janata (T), Larry Kubin (LB), 74 Gene Sanders (T), 63 Lee Roy Selmon (DE)

Prediction

'You don't ever really want to hold the first pick in the college draft,' said Tampa's head coach Leeman Bennet, 'because it means the year just passed was not successful. But hold it we do and we feel that that, along with the other selections we have, will enable us to significantly speed up the process of building our team.'

Play-off prediction

0

Washington Redskins

NATIONAL FOOTBALL CONFERENCE — EASTERN DIVISION

Address:	Redskin Park, PO Box 17247, Dulles International Airport, Washington, D.C. 20041
Telephone:	(703) 471-9100
Colours:	Burgundy and gold
Stadium:	Robert F. Kennedy Stadium, East Capitol Street, Washington, D.C. 20003
Capacity:	55,431
Playing surface:	Grass

History

Who boasted, 'Ron may be President but for tonight I'm King'? Well, it was John Riggins (the old Diesel) and the night was 30 January 1983. Riggo had been voted the most valuable player in Superbowl XVII, and the Redskins became Lord of the Rings, winning the Vince Lombardi Trophy. And what a night that was — coach Joe Gibbs was telephoned by President Reagan (it was televised, of course) as the Redskins beat the Dolphins 27-17, and earned their first world title in forty years.

The Redskins scored their first major win way back in 1937 against the Chicago Bears in icy conditions on a frozen field. The score, 28-21. Three years later in 1940, the Redskins won the Eastern Championship 13-6 and the World Championship was theirs again in 1942. The Bears had taken an early lead, and looked set to repeat their massive and humiliating 1940 World

Championship victory over the Redskins (73-0 at Griffith Park) but coach Ray Flaherty, by simply writing a large '73-0' on the blackboard in the Washington dressingroom, motivated his team to a convincing 14-6 triumph — stopping the Bears' undefeated string at 18. Champs again in 1943, the Redskins took the Eastern title, thrashing the New York Giants 28-0, and yet again in 1945 beating the Giants 17-0. In 1961 the Redskins moved to the J.F.K. Stadium in Washington, D.C. The first game in their new home, in front of a crowd of 37,767, was a sad defeat with the Redskins failing to hold their 21-0 lead and the Giants winning 24-21.

In 1965 the great Sonny Jurgensen, passing for over 400 yards and with three touchdowns, sparked the greatest comeback win in Redskin history. Down 21-0, the Redskins went on to record a 34-31 victory over the Dallas Cowboys. In 1966, a game between the Redskins and the Giants produced the most points in NFL history: a total of 113, with the Redskins scoring 72 of them. Sonny had his best season throwing 436 times, and completed 254 for 3,209 yards and 28 touchdowns.

The unbelievable happened in 1969 when Vince Lombardi left Green Bay to become part-owner, executive vice-president and head coach of the Redskins. His record of never having coached a losing NFL team was kept intact when the Redskins defeated New Orleans 17-14 — their first winning season since 1955! But less than a year later, just two weeks before the start of the season, Lombardi died.

Winning the NFC Championships in 1972, the Redskins took their first title in 30 years — a convincing 26-3 win over defending Champions, the Dallas Cowboys. But they lost Superbowl VII, 14-7 to the Miami Dolphins. Eleven years later they grasped their chance to drown the Dolphins 27-17 to take Superbowl XVII.

They looked set the following year to join the elite club of Green Bay, Miami and Pittsburgh, the only three teams to have won consecutive Superbowls. In a thrilling NFC Championship game they narrowly beat the San Francisco 49ers 24-21. It was a game that many said the 49ers should have won but luck was on Washington's side... though not for long. The Redskins arrived in Florida for Superbowl XVIII. Joe Theisman and his team never really got into gear against an intimidating Raiders

Washington Redskins vs NFL

	Won	Lost	Tied
Atlanta	9	2	1
Buffalo	2	2	0
Chicago	11	20	1
Cincinnati	3	1	0
Cleveland	8	31	1
Dallas	20	30	2
Denver	2	1	0
Detroit	19	8	0
Green Bay	11	14	1
Houston	2	2	0
Indianapolis	6	15	0
Kansas City	1	2	0
Los Angeles Raiders	1	4	0
Los Angeles Rams	14	5	1
Miami	2	4	0
Minnesota	4	5	0
New England	3	1	0
New Orleans	7	4	0
New York Giants	46	58	3
New York Jets	3	0	0
Philadelphia	57	39	5
Pittsburgh	40	27	3
San Diego	3	0	0
San Francisco	6	8	1
St Louis	49	32	2
Seattle	2	1	0
Tampa Bay	2	0	0

team hellbent on taking the Vince Lombardi Trophy back to Tinseltown. In what was then the largest margin of victory in a Superbowl, the Raiders scalped the Redskins 38-9.

End-of-season depth chart

OFFENSE

WR	— 84 Gary Clark, 83 Mark McGrath, 80 Joe Phillips
OTE	— 86 Clint Didier, 88 Rick Walker
OLT	— 66 Joe Jacoby, 60 Dan McQuaid, 68 Russ Grimm
OLG	— 68 Russ Grimm, 53 Jeff Bostic, 63 Raleigh McKenzie
C	— 53 Jeff Bostic, 76 Rick Donnalley, 63 Russ Grimm
ORG	— 61 Ken Huff, 53 Jeff Bostic, 63 Raleigh McKenzie
ORT	— 73 Mark May, 60 Dan McQuaid
TE	— 85 Don Warren, 82 Anthony Jones
WR	— 81 Art Monk, 83 Mark McGrath, 80 Joe Phillips
QB	— 10 Jay Schroeder, 16 Babe Laufenberg, 17 Steve Bartkowski
RB	— 38 George Rogers, 44 John Riggins, 35 Keith Griffin, 39 Otis Wonsley, 30 Reggie Branch

DEFENSE

DLE	— 71 Charles Mann, 64 Steve Hamilton
DLT	— 65 Dave Butz, 67 Tom Beasley
DRT	— 78 Dean Hamel, 67 Tom Beasley
DRE	— 72 Dexter Manley, 64 Steve Hamilton
LLB	— 55 Mel Kaufman, 51 Monte Coleman, 58 Stuart Anderson
MLB	— 52 Neal Olkewicz, 57 Rich Milot
RLB	— 57 Rich Milot, 51 Monte Coleman, 58 Stuart Anderson
LCB	— 28 Darrell Green, 45 Barry Wilburn, 34 Kevin Williams
RCB	— 32 Vernon Dean, 45 Barry Wilburn, 34 Kevin Williams
SS	— 37 Raphel Cherry, 22 Curtis Jordan, 23 Tony Peters
FS	— 22 Curtis Jordan, 37 Raphael Cherry, 47 Greg Williams

SPECIAL TEAMS

P	— 12 Steve Cox, 10 Jay Schroeder
K	— 3 Mark Moseley, 12 Steve Cox
H	— 10 Jay Schroeder, 12 Steve Cox
PR	— 28 Darrell Green, 84 Gary Clark, 37 Raphel Cherry
KR	— 35 Keith Griffin, 37 Raphel Cherry, 39 Otis Wonsley
LSN	— 53 Jeff Bostic, 60 Dan McQuaid

ALSO WITH THE WASHINGTON REDSKINS
48 Ken Coffey (S), Darnell Dailey (LB), 77 Darryl Grant (DT), 5 Jeff Hayes (P), Ken Jenkins (RB/KR), Bruce Kimball (G), Danzell Lee (TE), Mike McClearn (T), 89 Calvin Muhammad (WR), Mike Newton (RB), Terry Orr (TE), Chris Osswald (C/G), Willie Roseborough (DE), Bob Slater (DT), 7 Joe Theismann (QB), 69 R.C. Thielemann (G), Lionel Vital (RB)

Last season

The Redskins did well to finish 10-6, after the twin blows of losing three of their first four outings and quarterback Joe Theisman through injury. But back-up quarterback Jay Schroeder stepped into the breach and kept the ship on course with some tidy play. Running back George Rogers took a while to settle in (who could blame him?) but started to make his mark as the season progressed.

In the air, Art Monk was again one of the best, while USFL refugee Gary Clark fitted in well. And tight end Clint Didier always seemed to be the man they turned to when the chips were down.

The defense performed consistently throughout, although mention should be made of Dexter Manley, Neal Olkewicz and Curtis Jordan. Washington never really looked like repeating their Superbowl win, but coach Joe Gibbs has obviously planned for the future. The heart of the Superbowl side is still beating.

Prediction

With the twin departures of Joe Theisman and John Riggins, the Redskins' approach is bound to change. It was rumoured last year that some Redskins were secretly quite pleased that they had a new quarterback and although we should see them in the play-offs this year it is difficult to visualize them in the Superbowl... Give them a couple of years, though...

Play-off prediction

8

Schedule for 1986 Season

(All times local)

		KICKOFF	SCORE
SUNDAY, 7 SEPTEMBER (First Weekend)			
1	Atlanta at New Orleans	12.00	
2	Cincinnati at Kansas City	3.00	
3	Cleveland at Chicago	12.00	
4	Detroit at Minnesota	12.00	
5	Houston at Green Bay	12.00	
6	Indianapolis at New England	4.00	
7	Los Angeles Raiders at Denver	2.00	
8	Los Angeles Rams at St Louis	12.00	
9	Miami at San Diego	1.00	
10	New York Jets at Buffalo	4.00	
11	Philadelphia at Washington	1.00	
12	Pittsburgh at Seattle	1.00	
13	San Francisco at Tampa Bay	1.00	
MONDAY, 8 SEPTEMBER			
14	New York Giants at Dallas	8.00	
THURSDAY, 11 SEPTEMBER (Second Weekend)			
15	New England at New York Jets	8.00	
SUNDAY, 14 SEPTEMBER			
16	Buffalo at Cincinnati	1.00	
17	Cleveland at Houston	12.00	
18	Dallas at Detroit	1.00	
19	Green Bay at New Orleans	12.00	
20	Indianapolis at Miami	4.00	
21	Kansas City at Seattle	1.00	
22	Los Angeles Raiders at Washington	1.00	
23	Minnesota at Tampa Bay	4.00	
24	Philadelphia at Chicago	12.00	
25	St Louis at Atlanta	1.00	

		KICKOFF	SCORE
26	San Diego at New York Giants	1.00	
27	San Francisco at Los Angeles Rams	1.00	

MONDAY, 15 SEPTEMBER

| 28 | Denver at Pittsburgh | 9.00 | |

THURSDAY, 18 SEPTEMBER (Third Weekend)

| 29 | Cincinnati at Cleveland | 8.00 | |

SUNDAY, 21 SEPTEMBER

30	Atlanta at Dallas	12.00	
31	Denver at Philadelphia	1.00	
32	Houston at Kansas City	3.00	
33	Los Angeles Rams at Indianapolis	12.00	
34	Miami at New York Jets	1.00	
35	New Orleans at San Francisco	1.00	
36	New York Giants at Los Angeles Raiders	1.00	
37	Pittsburgh at Minnesota	12.00	
38	St Louis at Buffalo	1.00	
39	Seattle at New England	1.00	
40	Tampa Bay at Detroit	1.00	
41	Washington at San Diego	1.00	

MONDAY, 22 SEPTEMBER

| 42 | Chicago at Green Bay | 8.00 | |

SUNDAY, 28 SEPTEMBER (Fourth Weekend)

43	Atlanta at Tampa Bay	4.00	
44	Chicago at Cincinnati	1.00	
45	Detroit at Cleveland	1.00	
46	Green Bay at Minnesota	12.00	
47	Kansas City at Buffalo	1.00	
48	Los Angeles Rams at Philadelphia	1.00	
49	New England at Denver	2.00	
50	New Orleans at New York Giants	1.00	
51	New York Jets at Indianapolis	3.00	
52	Pittsburgh at Houston	12.00	
53	San Diego at Los Angeles Raiders	1.00	
54	San Francisco at Miami	1.00	
55	Seattle at Washington	1.00	

MONDAY, 29 SEPTEMBER

| 56 | Dallas at St Louis | 8.00 | |

SUNDAY, 5 OCTOBER (Fifth Weekend)

57	Buffalo at New York Jets	4.00
58	Cincinnati vs Green Bay at Milwaukee	12.00
59	Cleveland at Pittsburgh	1.00
60	Dallas at Denver	2.00
61	Houston at Detroit	1.00
62	Indianapolis at San Francisco	1.00
63	Los Angeles Raiders at Kansas City	12.00
64	Miami at New England	1.00
65	Minnesota at Chicago	12.00
66	New York Giants at St Louis	12.00
67	Philadelphia at Atlanta	1.00
68	Tampa Bay at Los Angeles Rams	1.00
69	Washington at New Orleans	12.00

MONDAY, 6 OCTOBER

70	San Diego at Seattle	6.00

SUNDAY, 12 OCTOBER (Sixth Weekend)

71	Buffalo at Miami	1.00
72	Chicago at Houston	12.00
73	Denver at San Diego	1.00
74	Detroit at Green Bay	12.00
75	Kansas City at Cleveland	1.00
76	Los Angeles Rams at Atlanta	1.00
77	Minnesota at San Francisco	1.00
78	New Orleans at Indianapolis	12.00
79	New York Jets at New England	1.00
80	Philadelphia at New York Giants	4.00
81	St Louis at Tampa Bay	1.00
82	Seattle at Los Angeles Raiders	1.00
83	Washington at Dallas	12.00

MONDAY, 13 OCTOBER

84	Pittsburgh at Cincinnati	9.00

SUNDAY, 19 OCTOBER (Seventh Weekend)

85	Chicago at Minnesota	12.00
86	Dallas at Philadelphia	1.00
87	Detroit at Los Angeles Rams	1.00
88	Green Bay at Cleveland	1.00
89	Houston at Cincinnati	1.00
90	Indianapolis at Buffalo	1.00
91	Los Angeles Raiders at Miami	1.00

		KICKOFF	**SCORE**
92	New England at Pittsburgh	1.00	
93	New York Giants at Seattle	1.00	
94	St Louis at Washington	1.00	
95	San Diego at Kansas City	3.00	
96	San Francisco at Atlanta	1.00	
97	Tampa Bay at New Orleans	12.00	

MONDAY, 20 OCTOBER

98	Denver at New York Jets	9.00

SUNDAY, 26 OCTOBER (Eighth Weekend)

99	Atlanta at Los Angeles Rams	1.00
100	Cincinnati at Pittsburgh	1.00
101	Cleveland at Minnesota	12.00
102	Detroit at Chicago	12.00
103	Los Angeles Raiders at Houston	12.00
104	Miami at Indianapolis	1.00
105	New England at Buffalo	1.00
106	New Orleans at New York Jets	1.00
107	St Louis at Dallas	3.00
108	San Diego at Philadelphia	1.00
109	San Francisco vs Green Bay at Milwaukee	12.00
110	Seattle at Denver	2.00
111	Tampa Bay at Kansas City	12.00

MONDAY, 27 OCTOBER

112	Washington at New York Giants	9.00

SUNDAY, 2 NOVEMBER (Ninth Weekend)

113	Atlanta at New England	1.00
114	Buffalo at Tampa Bay	1.00
115	Cincinnati at Detroit	1.00
116	Cleveland at Indianapolis	1.00
117	Dallas at New York Giants	1.00
118	Denver at Los Angeles Raiders	1.00
119	Green Bay at Pittsburgh	1.00
120	Houston at Miami	1.00
121	Kansas City at San Diego	1.00
122	Minnesota at Washington	4.00
123	New York Jets at Seattle	1.00
124	Philadelphia at St Louis	12.00
125	San Francisco at New Orleans	12.00

MONDAY, 3 NOVEMBER

126	Los Angeles Rams at Chicago	8.00

		KICKOFF	SCORE

SUNDAY, 9 NOVEMBER (Tenth Weekend)

127	Chicago at Tampa Bay	1.00	
128	Cincinnati at Houston	12.00	
129	Los Angeles Raiders at Dallas	3.00	
130	Los Angeles Rams at New Orleans	12.00	
131	Minnesota at Detroit	1.00	
132	New England at Indianapolis	1.00	
133	New York Giants at Philadelphia	4.00	
134	New York Jets at Atlanta	1.00	
135	Pittsburgh at Buffalo	1.00	
136	St Louis at San Francisco	1.00	
137	San Diego at Denver	2.00	
138	Seattle at Kansas City	12.00	
139	Washington at Green Bay	12.00	

MONDAY, 10 NOVEMBER

140	Miami at Cleveland	9.00	

SUNDAY, 16 NOVEMBER (Eleventh Weekend)

141	Chicago at Atlanta	1.00	
142	Cleveland at Los Angeles Raiders	1.00	
143	Dallas at San Diego	1.00	
144	Detroit at Philadelphia	1.00	
145	Houston at Pittsburgh	1.00	
146	Indianapolis at New York Jets	4.00	
147	Kansas City at Denver	2.00	
148	New England at Los Angeles Rams	1.00	
149	Miami at Buffalo	1.00	
150	New York Giants at Minnesota	12.00	
151	New Orleans at St Louis	12.00	
152	Seattle at Cincinnati	1.00	
153	Tampa Bay vs Green Bay at Milwaukee	12.00	

MONDAY, 17 NOVEMBER

154	San Francisco at Washington	9.00	

THURSDAY, 20 NOVEMBER (Twelfth Weekend)

155	Los Angeles Raiders at San Diego	5.00	

SUNDAY, 23 NOVEMBER

156	Atlanta at San Francisco	1.00	
157	Buffalo at New England	1.00	
158	Dallas at Washington	1.00	

189

		KICKOFF	SCORE
159	Denver at New York Giants	1.00	
160	Detroit at Tampa Bay	1.00	
161	Green Bay at Chicago	12.00	
162	Indianapolis at Houston	12.00	
163	Kansas City at St Louis	3.00	
164	Minnesota at Cincinnati	1.00	
165	New Orleans at Los Angeles Rams	1.00	
166	Philadelphia at Seattle	1.00	
167	Pittsburgh at Cleveland	1.00	

MONDAY, 24 NOVEMBER

168	New York Jets at Miami	9.00	

THURSDAY, 27 NOVEMBER (Thirteenth Weekend)
(Thanksgiving Day)

169	Green Bay at Detroit	12.30	
170	Seattle at Dallas	3.00	

SUNDAY, 30 NOVEMBER

171	Atlanta at Miami	1.00	
172	Buffalo at Kansas City	12.00	
173	Cincinnati at Denver	2.00	
174	Houston at Cleveland	1.00	
175	Los Angeles Rams at New York Jets	1.00	
176	New England at New Orleans	12.00	
177	Philadelphia at Los Angeles Raiders	1.00	
178	Pittsburgh at Chicago	12.00	
179	San Diego at Indianapolis	1.00	
180	Tampa Bay at Minnesota	12.00	
181	Washington at St Louis	12.00	

MONDAY, 1 DECEMBER

182	New York Giants at San Francisco	6.00	

SUNDAY, 7 DECEMBER (Fourteenth Weekend)

183	Cincinnati at New England	1.00	
184	Cleveland at Buffalo	1.00	
185	Dallas at Los Angeles Rams	6.00	
186	Denver at Kansas City	12.00	
187	Detroit at Pittsburgh	1.00	
188	Houston at San Diego	1.00	
189	Indianapolis at Atlanta	1.00	
190	Miami at New Orleans	12.00	
191	Minnesota at Green Bay	12.00	

		KICKOFF	SCORE
192	New York Giants at Washington	1.00	
193	New York Jets at San Francisco	1.00	
194	St Louis at Philadelphia	1.00	
195	Tampa Bay at Chicago	12.00	

MONDAY, 8 DECEMBER

196	Los Angeles Raiders at Seattle	6.00	

SATURDAY, 13 DECEMBER (Fifteenth Weekend)

197	Pittsburgh at New York Jets	12.30	
198	Washington at Denver	2.00	

SUNDAY, 14 DECEMBER

199	Buffalo at Indianapolis	1.00	
200	Cleveland at Cincinnati	1.00	
201	Green Bay at Tampa Bay	1.00	
202	Kansas City at Los Angeles Raiders	1.00	
203	Miami at Los Angeles Rams	1.00	
204	Minnesota at Houston	3.00	
205	New Orleans at Atlanta	1.00	
206	Philadelphia at Dallas	12.00	
207	St Louis at New York Giants	1.00	
208	San Francisco at New England	1.00	
209	Seattle at San Diego	1.00	

MONDAY, 15 DECEMBER

210	Chicago at Detroit	9.00	

FRIDAY, 19 DECEMBER (Sixteenth Weekend)

211	Los Angeles Rams at San Francisco	5.00	

SATURDAY, 20 DECEMBER

212	Denver at Seattle	1.00	
213	Green Bay at New York Giants	12.30	

SUNDAY, 21 DECEMBER

214	Atlanta at Detroit	1.00	
215	Buffalo at Houston	12.00	
216	Chicago at Dallas	3.00	
217	Indianapolis at Los Angeles Raiders	1.00	
218	Kansas City at Pittsburgh	1.00	
219	New Orleans at Minnesota	12.00	
220	New York Jets at Cincinnati	1.00	

		KICKOFF	SCORE
221	San Diego at Cleveland	1.00	
222	Tampa Bay at St Louis	12.00	
223	Washington at Philadelphia	1.00	

MONDAY, 22 DECEMBER

224	New England at Miami	9.00